CULTURE SMART!

BRITAIN

THE ESSENTIAL GUIDE TO CUSTOMS & CULTURE

SARAH RICHES

KUPERARD

"The real voyage of discovery consists not in seeking new landscapes, but in having new eyes."

Adapted from Marcel Proust, *Remembrance of Things Past.*

ISBN 978 1 78702 357 4

British Library Cataloguing in Publication Data
A CIP catalogue entry for this book is available
from the British Library

First published in Great Britain
by Kuperard, an imprint of Bravo Ltd
59 Hutton Grove, London N12 8DS
Tel: +44 (0) 20 8446 2440
www.culturesmart.co.uk
Inquiries: publicity@kuperard.co.uk

Design Bobby Birchall
Printed in Turkey

The Culture Smart! series is continuing to expand.
All Culture Smart! guides are available as e-books, and many
as audio books. For further information and latest titles visit
www.culturesmart.co.uk

ABOUT THE AUTHOR

SARAH RICHES is an English travel writer based in London. On graduating from Lancaster University, she spent the next five years traveling in Japan, Hong Kong, and Taiwan. After climbing the Great Wall of China, sailing in Ha Long Bay in Vietnam, and hot air ballooning at sunrise over Angkor Wat in Cambodia, she returned to England to study Magazine Journalism at City, University of London.

Sarah is particularly interested in local and indigenous cultures, and has written for *National Geographic Traveller*, *Condé Nast Traveller*, *Wanderlust*, *Where London*, *London Planner*, *Travel Almanac*, and www.adventure.com. She has edited magazines, hosted writing courses, written the guidebook *London Almanac,* co-written *Time Out's Eating Out in Abu Dhabi*, and worked on *The Wanderlust World Travel Quiz Book*. She is now the editor of *World Cruising*.

When not traveling abroad, Sarah explores Britain on day trips and weekends away—particularly the Isle of Wight, the Cotswolds, Cornwall, and the creative hubs along England's south coast.

CONTENTS

INTRODUCTION

Situated on the western edge of continental Europe, the British Isles have had a global impact out of all proportion to their modest size. Strongly rooted in their ancient traditions, the British people have also been remarkably open to influences from other cultures.

Britain's thirty-three UNESCO World Heritage Sites offer insights into life here during the Neolithic era, the Roman Empire, the Norman Conquest, and the more recent past. They are also tangible examples of the respect Britain has for its heritage.

Pride in the past is evident in the spectacular opening ceremony of the Olympic Summer Games in London in 2012, in the pomp and pageantry of state occasions such as the Coronation of King Charles in 2023, and in the continuing high ratings of TV period dramas.

As a family of nations, Britain is home to an inventive, reflective, good-humored, funny, focused, and tenacious people—qualities that have led to remarkable outcomes: the largest empire in history, a centuries-old trade network, a monarchy that has lasted more than a thousand years, and a parliamentary democracy and justice system that have been a template for the world.

The peculiar character of the British has always intrigued visitors, who have described them variously as enigmatic, idiosyncratic, eccentric, reserved, and quaint—all of which contain a certain amount of truth. Britain also has a reputation abroad for being insular and different, sometimes frustratingly so.

The country has produced some of the world's greatest museums, theater, art, and literature; kickstarted the Industrial Revolution; conceived most of the world's major sports, from golf and rugby to cricket and football; and invented countless items of technology that have advanced the quality of life. It has won more Nobel Prizes than the rest of Europe combined, and connected the world through the English language.

Britain's influence today has changed, and perhaps declined. Yet it remains the world's sixth-largest economy, and its creative culture and entrepreneurial spirit, particularly in London, continues to attract and fascinate visitors.

In recent years Britain has witnessed unimagined and accelerated change, from leaving the EU following the 2016 vote for Brexit to dealing with the 2020 Covid-19 pandemic, and with the new hybrid-working revolution that has taken place since. There's constant speculation about the shape of the country's future—particularly because of the climate crisis, the impact of Russia's invasion of Ukraine, the growing influence of China, and the lack of post-Brexit trade deals.

What can be said with certainty, however, is that Britons will cope with the challenges they face. They will make do, muddle through, and somehow accommodate and adapt in order to secure the future and keep their traditions and values, such as politeness, free health care provision, and perseverance, largely intact. After all, Britain's motto since the Second World War has been "Keep calm and carry on."

This updated edition of *Culture Smart! Britain* aims to help you gain more from your stay in these islands through a greater understanding of the quirks, customs, values, and changing ways of British life.

Official Name	The United Kingdom of Great Britain and Northern Ireland	Member of NATO, G7, G8, the UN Security Council, and the Organisation for Economic Co-operation and Development
Capital Cities	London (population 8.7 million)	Other capitals: Edinburgh, Cardiff, Belfast
Other Main Cities	England: *Birmingham, Manchester, Liverpool.* Scotland: *Glasgow, Aberdeen.* Wales: *Swansea, Wrexham, Newport.* Northern Ireland: *Derry/Londonderry*	
Area	Total area approx. 93,832 sq. miles (243,025 sq. km). *England:* 50,318 sq.miles (130,324 sq. km); *Scotland:* 30,297 sq. miles (78,469 sq. km); *Wales:* 8,021 sq. miles (20,774 sq. km); *N. Ireland:* 5,196 sq. miles (13,458 sq. km)	
Climate	Temperate. The Isles of Scilly range from 6–10°C (42–50°F) in winter to 11–19°C (51–66°F) in summer; Braemar in Aberdeenshire ranges from -1–4°C in winter to 7–18°C (44–64°F) in summer.	
Population	67 million. England 56.5 million; Scotland 5.5 million; Wales 3.1 million; N. Ireland 1.9 million	Population under 25 in England and Wales: 29%. Population over 60 in England and Wales: 24%
Ethnic Makeup	White: 81.7% in England and Wales, 96% in Scotland, 96.6% in N. Ireland	Main ethnic minorities: Indian, Pakistani, Black African, Black Caribbean
Family Makeup	Average members per household: 2.3	
Religion	Church of England, Churches of Wales and Scotland (Protestant), Roman Catholic	Principal minority religions: Judaism, Hinduism, Islam, Sikhism

Language	English	English and Welsh in Wales, Scottish Gaelic, Cornish
Government	Constitutional monarchy. No written constitution: the relationship between state and people is based on statute law, common law, and conventions.	Parliament consists of two chambers, the elected House of Commons and unelected House of Lords, and is the supreme authority of government and law-making.
Currency	Pound Sterling	Symbol: £
Press	Broadsheets: *The Daily Telegraph / The Sunday Telegraph, The Guardian / The Observer*, and *The Times / The Sunday Times*	Tabloids: *Daily Mail / The Mail on Sunday, Daily Mirror / Sunday Mirror, Daily Star / Daily Star Sunday, Daily Express, The Sun / The Sun on Sunday*, and the *Sunday People*
Broadcasting	The main terrestrial channels are BBC One, BBC Two, ITV, and Channel 4. 96% of British households have internet access.	On-demand streaming services include Amazon Prime Video, Apple TV+, Disney+, Netflix, NOW, BritBox, DAZN, Hayu, and Sky.
Electricity	230 volts, 50 Hz	
Telephone	Britain's country code is 44.	Cell phone providers include Asda Mobile, EE, giffgaff, Three, Tesco Mobile, O2, Orange and Sky, Virgin Mobile, and Vodaphone.
Time Zone	Greenwich Mean Time (GMT)	British Summer Time = GMT + 1 hr

CHAPTER ONE

LAND & PEOPLE

WHAT IS "BRITAIN"?

Confused about the difference between Britain, Great Britain, the United Kingdom, the UK, and England? You're not alone. "Great Britain"—which is often abbreviated to "Britain"—comprises England, Wales, and Scotland, as well as offshore islands, including the Isle of Wight, the Isles of Scilly, the Hebrides, Orkney, and the Shetlands. The "United Kingdom" (UK) meanwhile consists of Great Britain and Northern Ireland, which shares a land border with the Republic of Ireland. The Isle of Man in the Irish Sea, and the Channel Islands in the English Channel between Britain and France, are known as Crown Dependencies. They are not part of the UK and are largely self-governing.

The "British Isles" is essentially a geographical term used to describe all of the above plus the whole of the island of Ireland, as well as the Isle of Man and the Channel Islands.

Britain is located on the western edge of the continental shelf of Europe. It consists of two large islands and several hundred smaller ones that were separated from the European continent in about 6000 BCE. The mild maritime climate and undulating lowlands give the mainland an excellent agricultural base. The landscape becomes increasingly mountainous toward the north, rising to the Cambrian Mountains in Wales, the Pennines in northern England, and the Grampian Mountains in Scotland. Major rivers include the Thames in the south, the Severn in the west, and the Spey in Scotland.

CLIMATE

Britain's climate is often thought of as cool, wet, cloudy, and windswept. This generalization, however, fails to take account of microclimates or regional variations in weather. Climate change is also blurring the distinctions of the seasons, especially the autumn (fall)–winter–spring periods. The British weather overall is controlled mainly by a series of depressions from the Atlantic that move across or pass near the British Isles on account of the prevailing southwesterly wind.

Given the considerable variations in Britain's weather, it is a constant topic of conversation. Freak weather events, from catastrophic flooding to extreme heat, occupy the headlines for days. Weather commentators insist on stating that it was the hottest, wettest, coldest "since records began," which actually only takes us back to 1914 (under the control of the Meteorological Office), although there are records for England going back to 1766 and even earlier if you include those of amateur meteorologists.

Historically, there have been many recorded "freak" conditions. For example, on January 21, 1661, five years before the Great Fire of London, Samuel Pepys recorded in his diary: "It is strange what weather we have had all this winter; no cold at all, but the ways are dusty, and the flyes fly up and down, and rose bushes are full of leaves . . ." On the other hand, in 1683 and 1771, the Thames River froze, forming a natural ice rink.

So, although Britain tends to be cloudy and overcast, only about half the country has more than 30 inches (76 cm) of rain annually—except in the past ten or fifteen years, as noted above, when freak flooding has overturned the precipitation tables. The wettest areas are Snowdonia, with about 200 inches (508 cm) of rain, and the Lake District, much loved by tourists, with 132 inches (335 cm). The wettest city is Glasgow with 170 rainy days (average) and the driest is Cambridge with only 107 wet days per year.

England enjoys the best weather overall, especially in the southwest, which benefits from being in the path of the Gulf Stream (as do the Western Isles of Scotland). The coldest parts of Britain are the Scottish Highlands. On top of Ben Nevis, the highest peak, the mean temperature for the year is around the freezing point, while many north-facing gullies contain year-round snow. Air temperatures seldom rise above 90°F (32°C) or drop below 14°F (-10°C).

WHO ARE THE BRITISH?

Politically, the peoples of the United Kingdom of Great Britain and Northern Ireland, including the indigenous English, Scots, Irish, and Welsh, those from former colonies, and the many others who have made Britain their home, are called "British." On the other hand, it is important to understand that the cultural traditions of the British, particularly the Celtic, Anglo-Saxon, Nordic, and Norman French cultures, remain at the center of the traditional "British way of life."

The centuries of conflict that were finally resolved in the Act of Union uniting the governments of England and Scotland in 1707 (the monarchies having united a hundred years earlier, in 1603) generated a profound and, at times, fiercely defended sense of separate identity. This is, perhaps, best demonstrated in the national football and rugby teams for England, Scotland, Wales, and Northern Ireland. The matches between the four nations—especially World Cup games—are typically fought with passion, above all because they are a matter of national pride. A 2014 referendum on Scottish independence also resulted in a surge of Scottish nationalism. Voter turnout was a record-breaking 84.59 percent. Although those in favor of retaining the Union won by a margin of 10 percent, the Scottish independence movement grew stronger after the United Kingdom voted in a 2016 referendum to leave the European Union.

In addition to Britain's indigenous cultures, the nation also includes what could be called its

"Empire" cultures—principally from the Indian subcontinent, Africa, and the Caribbean.

In the most recent Census (2021), the UK population was estimated to be 67 million. The census that year revealed that 81.7 percent of residents in England and Wales identified as White—lower than the 86 percent recorded in the 2011 census. In Scotland, the percentage was higher; its 2011 census found that 96 percent of the population was White.

The largest ethnic minority in England and Wales—those who identify as Asian, Asian British, or Asian Welsh—stood at 9.3 percent (5.5 million) in 2021, up from 7.5 percent (4.2 million) a decade earlier. In Scotland, the 2011 census revealed Polish, Irish, Gypsy/Traveler, or White Other to be the largest ethnic minority there, at 4.2 percent.

Black, Black British, Black Welsh, Caribbean, or African make up the second-largest ethnic minority in England and Wales; the 2021 census recorded 2.5 percent (1.5 million)—another rise from the previous census, which recorded 1.8 percent (990,000). The Scottish 2011 census found 4 percent of the population to be Asian, African, Caribbean, Black, Mixed, or another ethnic group.

Following protests in Hong Kong against a 2019 bill that would allow extraditions to mainland China, the return of the Taliban to power in Afghanistan in 2021, and the Russian invasion of Ukraine in 2022, the UK government introduced schemes to welcome people from Hong Kong, Afghanistan, and Ukraine. These diasporas will likely be reflected in future censuses.

New communities are not evenly spread across the country, creating a mixed pattern of integration and cohesion. For example, about two-thirds of Black ethnic groups live in London. In Leicester, Wolverhampton, and Birmingham, there are large numbers of Indians, and many Pakistanis and Bangladeshis live in Birmingham, Greater Manchester, and West Yorkshire, especially in Leeds and Bradford.

More than four-fifths of the UK's total population live in England. The greatest concentrations of people are in London (8.7 million in 2021) and the Southeast, South and West Yorkshire, Greater Manchester and Merseyside, the West Midlands, and adjoining towns in the Northeast on the rivers Tyne (Newcastle), Wear (Durham and Sunderland), and Tees (Middlesbrough).

Since the 1976 Race Relations Act, the 2010 Equality Act, and the establishment of the Equality and Human Rights Commission, the government has actively promoted a policy affirming the multiracial nature of British society. While such legislation is not universally welcome, it is generally accepted. Britain's cities are largely multiracial and multicultural, and life is all the more colorful and vibrant for it; but traditional town or village life in Britain is still far from this.

THE SHAPING OF BRITAIN

The British character has been formed by the accident of geography and two thousand years of history. Successive invasions left their mark, the native peoples jostled for power, and collectively the British burst beyond the confines of their borders on to the world scene. At the end of this chapter is a list of significant dates in British history. First, however, we look at the early centuries that laid the foundations for the culture and way of life of today's Britain.

In 55 and 54 BCE the Roman general and statesman Julius Caesar, when proconsul of Gaul, led expeditions to reconnoiter Britain for potential resources and settlement. Nearly a hundred years later, in 43 CE, the Emperor Claudius invaded and conquered Britain, ushering in three-hundred and fifty years of Roman rule.

Marble bust of Julius Caesar by Andrea Ferrucci.

By the beginning of the fifth century, however, the Roman Empire was in decline, resulting in the virtual collapse of many of its outposts, including Britain. The last remnants of the Roman army withdrew in c. 409 CE.

With the Romans no longer maintaining law and order, Celtic Britain was soon at the mercy of marauding Germanic tribes—the Jutes (Hengist and Horsa), the Saxons, and the Angles. The Roman-style civil governments that were left continued to beg Rome, in vain, for help against the invaders. Eventually, England was overrun and became a predominantly Anglo-Saxon society, with the indigenous Celtic peoples pushed to the extremities—Cornwall, Wales, Scotland, and the island of Ireland.

At the end of the eighth century, however, a new wave of invaders traumatized the people. This time, it was the sophisticated Norsemen—Viking pirates from Denmark, Norway, and Sweden—who wreaked havoc and destruction, at least initially, along vast areas of the British coast. The first of these devastating invasions was in 793 CE, when the great abbey of Lindisfarne in Northumbria—famous as a center of learning—was destroyed. The greatest Viking invasion, involving hundreds of ships—the biggest fleet England had ever seen—was to follow some seventy years later. This resulted in the fall of York in 867 CE.

Over time, the Vikings established authority in many parts of England. The administration of these areas became subject to what was known as Danelaw. Place names ending in *–by*, as in Whitby, and *–thorpe*, as in Scunthorpe, bear witness to their Viking past. Today, visitors can discover more about Viking life at the Jorvik Viking Centre in York, which brings to life the experience of the old city of Jorvik through moving models, sights, and smells.

Britain's next major milestone was in 1066, when it was last successfully invaded. William, Duke of Normandy, defeated the English at the Battle of Hastings on the south coast of England and became King William I, known as "William the Conqueror." The story of the battle is famously celebrated in the Bayeux Tapestry,

The Norman fleet crossing the Channel. Scene from the Bayeux Tapestry.

presumed to have been woven in Canterbury, and kept today in Bayeux, northwestern France.

Northern French became the language of the court and the ruling classes for the next three centuries, and French legal, social, and institutional practice greatly influenced the English way of life. When Henry II, originally from Anjou in France, was king (1154–89), his "Angevin empire" stretched from the Tweed River on the Scottish border, through much of France, to the Pyrenees. However, by the end of the Middle Ages (late fifteenth century), almost all the English Crown's possessions in France, after alternating periods of expansion and contraction, were finally lost.

England and Wales were brought together administratively and legally between 1536 and 1542 during the reign of Henry VIII (his family, the Tudors, had Welsh roots). After the death of Elizabeth I in 1603, James VI of Scotland (of the house of Stuart) became

Portrait of Queen Elizabeth I, commemorating the defeat of the Spanish Armada.

James I of England, uniting the two monarchies. The political union of England and Scotland took place in 1707, during the reign of Queen Anne—forming "Britain" as we know it today.

Britain's great overseas trading empire dates back to the reign of Elizabeth I (1558–1603), when the Queen sponsored opportunistic acts of piracy against the enemy, Spain. She appointed the privateer Francis Drake second-in-command of the British fleet that fought the Spanish Armada in 1588. During the eighteenth century, the navy expanded at the expense of its European rivals, making Britain the world's naval superpower in the nineteenth century. The parallel story of Britain's great social, technological, and cultural advances effectively maps the creation of the modern world.

KEY DATES

55 and 54 BCE Julius Caesar sends expeditions to England, landing at Pevensey, East Sussex.

43 CE Emperor Claudius and his 40,000 troops begin the Roman Conquest.

61 Boudicca (Boadicea), queen of the Iceni people, leads a rebellion against Rome. The Roman commander Paulinus crushes the revolt after overrunning London and St. Albans. Boudicca commits suicide the following year.

122–38 Running from the Solway to the Tyne, Hadrian's Wall is built to keep out marauding Scots (partly rebuilt 205–208).

314 British bishops attend the Council of Arles, providing evidence of an organized Church in Britain.

406–10 Britain loses its Roman forces.

449 Hengist and Horsa from Jutland invited to help fight the Picts. Later Jutes, Saxons, and Angles also land in Britain and begin establishing the Anglo-Saxon kingdoms.

597 The Pope sends the Roman prior St. Augustine to re-found Christianity in Britain. He becomes the first Archbishop of Canterbury.

664 Synod of Whitby chooses the Roman Catholic rather than the Celtic Church order.

789–95 First Viking raids, via Weymouth in southern England.

832–60 Scots and Picts merge under Kenneth MacAlpin to form what is to become the Kingdom of Scotland.

835 Egbert of Wessex is declared "King of the English."

851 Around 350 Danish ships attempt an invasion, and London and Canterbury are sacked.

860s Danes also overrun East Anglia, Northumbria, and eastern Mercia.

899 Alfred the Great, King of Wessex, dies.

1066 William, Duke of Normandy, invades England, defeats King Harold Godwinson near Hastings on October 14, and seizes the English throne.

1085–6 William I orders the compilation of the *Domesday Book*, a survey of English landholdings.

1170 Thomas à Becket, Archbishop of Canterbury, is murdered by supporters of Henry II on December 29.

1189 Richard I, "The Lion-Heart," is crowned, and sets out on the Third Crusade in 1191.

1215 King John is forced to sign Magna Carta at Runnymede. By protecting feudal rights from royal abuse, it set limits on royal power.

13th century: The first Oxford and Cambridge Colleges are founded. Edward of Caernarvon (later Edward II) becomes Prince of Wales.

1314 Robert the Bruce defeats the English at the Battle of Bannockburn, ensuring the survival of a separate Scottish kingdom.

1337 The Hundred Years War with France begins.

1348–9 The Black Death (bubonic plague) wipes out a third of England's population.

1381 Peasants' Revolt in England.

1387–94 Geoffrey Chaucer writes *The Canterbury Tales*.

1400–06 Owain Glyndwr (Owen Glendower) leads the last major Welsh revolt against English rule.

1411 St. Andrew's University is founded, becoming Scotland's first university.

1455–85 Wars of the Roses. Yorkists and Lancastrians fight for the English throne; the Lancastrians defeat Richard III at the Battle of Bosworth in 1485, and begin the Tudor dynasty with Henry VII.

1477 William Caxton prints the first book in England.

1534 Henry VIII formally breaks with Rome, founding the Church of England and setting in train the English Reformation.

1536–42 Acts of Union join England and Wales administratively and legally and give the Welsh representation in Parliament.

1547–53 Protestantism becomes the official religion of England under Edward VI.

1553–58 Mary I ("Bloody Mary") supports the return of Catholicism and burns Protestant "heretics" at the stake.

1558 England loses Calais, its last piece of French territory, to the French.

1558–1603 Reign of the "Virgin Queen," Elizabeth I, and the Golden Age of the Tudors.

1588 Spurred on by Elizabeth I's famous rallying speech, "I know I have the body of a weak and feeble woman, but I have the heart and stomach of a king …," a smaller English fleet defeats the Spanish Armada.

1590–1613 William Shakespeare writes his plays.

1603 The crowns of Scotland and England are united, when James VI of Scotland becomes James I of England.

1607 The first successful English colony in Virginia starts three centuries of overseas expansion.

1610 Plantation of Ulster. James I settles Northern Ireland with English and Scottish Protestants.

1642–51 A civil war between Charles I and Parliament breaks out.

1649 Charles I is executed on January 30 at Whitehall—the first and only British monarch to be executed with approval by the people (Parliament).

1653–58 Britain becomes a republic, the "Commonwealth," ruled by the Puritan Oliver Cromwell as Lord Protector. He abolishes the monarchy, the House of Lords, and the Anglican Church.

1660 The monarchy is restored under Charles II (1660–85), hence the Restoration Period (the Anglican Church and the House of Lords are also reinstated).

1662 The Royal Society for the Promotion of Natural Knowledge is founded.

1663 John Milton completes the poem "Paradise Lost."

1665 The Great Plague.

1666 The Great Fire of London begins in a baker's shop in Pudding Lane.

1686 Isaac Newton sets out his laws of motion and the idea of universal gravitation.

1689 The so-called "Glorious Revolution," a bloodless coup against the last Stuart monarch, James II, results in his expulsion and the coronation of William and Mary. Scottish Highlanders and Catholic Irish resist.

1707 Acts of Union unite the English and Scottish Parliaments.

1721–42 Robert Walpole becomes the first British Prime Minister.

1745–46 "Bonnie Prince Charlie" fails in his attempt to retake the British throne for the Stuarts.

1760–1840 The Industrial Revolution transforms Britain.

1761 The Bridgewater Canal opens from Worsley to Manchester and the River Mersey (42 miles, 67 km), kickstarting the Canal (transportation) Age.

1775–83 During the reign of George III (1760–1820), the American War of Independence leads to the loss of the Thirteen Colonies. The Empire continues to expand in Canada, India, and Australia.

1801 The Act of Union comes into force, uniting Britain and Ireland, governed by a single Parliament.

1805 Battle of Trafalgar. Nelson defeats the French navy. From his flagship *Victory* before the battle he sends the famous message, "England expects every man to do his duty."

1807 The Abolition of the Slave Trade Act ends the slave trade in the British Empire.

1815 Battle of Waterloo and final defeat of Napoleon Bonaparte.

1815–1914 A century of expansion of the Empire.

1825 Opening of the Stockton and Darlington Railway, the world's first passenger railway.

1829 Catholic emancipation allows Catholics to hold office legally and be elected to Parliament.

1832 The First Reform Act increases the number of those entitled to vote by 50 percent.

1833 The Slavery Abolition Act abolishes slavery in the British colonies.

1836–70 Charles Dickens writes his novels, starting with *The Pickwick Papers*; his last complete novel was *Our Mutual Friend* (1864); in the year of his death, 1870, he had begun *Edwin Drood*.

1837–1901 Queen Victoria reigns.

1846 The repeal of the Corn Laws shifts power from landowners to industrialists.

1859 Charles Darwin publishes *The Origin of Species by Means of Natural Selection*.

1868 The Trades Union Congress (TUC) is founded.

1907 Henry Royce and C. S. Rolls build and sell their first Rolls-Royce automobile, the "Silver Ghost."

1910–36 The Empire reaches its territorial zenith.

1914–18 First World War.

1918 Women win the right to vote.

1919–21 Anglo-Irish war. The Anglo-Irish Treaty establishes the Irish Free State; Northern Ireland (the Six Counties) remains part of the UK.

1924 Ramsay Macdonald leads the first Labour Government.

1926 A dispute over pay and conditions in the coal mines results in a General Strike.

1926 The Scottish inventor John Logie Baird gives the first practical demonstration of television.

1928 The Scottish physicist Alexander Fleming discovers penicillin.

1931 A national government coalition is formed to face the economic crisis.

1936 The Jarrow Crusade—the most famous of the 1930s' hunger marches.

1939–45 Second World War.

1943 The world's first electronic computer, "Colossus I," is built and used for breaking enemy codes in the Second World War.

1947 India and Pakistan win back their independence; Britain begins to dismantle the Empire.

1948 The NHS is established, offering free medical care to Britain's entire population.

1952 Elizabeth II ascends the throne.

1973 The UK joins the European Economic Community (EEC), the precursor to the EU.

1999 The Scottish Parliament (Pàrlamaid na h-Alba) and the National Assembly for Wales (now Senedd Cymru) are formed.

2012 London hosts the Olympic Summer Games, otherwise known as the Games of the XXX Olympiad.

2016 The UK votes to leave the EU.

2020 The UK goes into lockdown in response to the Covid-19 pandemic.

2022 Queen Elizabeth II, Britain's longest-serving monarch, dies aged ninety-six at Balmoral Castle.

2023 Queen Elizabeth II's eldest son becomes King Charles III following a Coronation Ceremony at Westminster Abbey.

Stonehenge, the iconic prehistoric stone structure on Salisbury Plain in Wlitshire.

HISTORICAL LANDMARKS

Britain has thousands of monuments, castles, and palaces, and the UK has thirty-three UNESCO World Heritage Sites—too many to mention here. A handful, however, offer an overview of British history.

UNESCO values the Heart of Neolithic Orkney—a neolithic settlement with two ceremonial stone circles, a chambered tomb, and other unexcavated burial sites—as it provides a depiction of life in Scotland c. 3000 BCE. The UNESCO-listed stone circles at Stonehenge and Avebury in southern England date back to roughly the same era.

The Romans meanwhile built the 73 mile (118 km)-long Hadrian's Wall across northern England on the orders of Emperor Hadrian in c. 122 CE. Another UNESCO site, it represents the Roman Empire's northernmost border.

Fast forward to the 1070s. During this time, the Tower of London was built for William the Conqueror after he successfully invaded England and became King William I.

More than two hundred years later, after his conquest of Wales, the English King Edward I ordered the construction of walls around Conwy and Caernarfon, and the building of Beaumaris, Conwy, Caernarfon, and Harlech castles.

Conwy Castle, built for Edward I by the master mason James of St. George from Savoy.

Famous Names

Many regions, towns, and cities are associated with specific British artists. London, of course, has always attracted creative talent. To take a few random examples, it is where J. M. W. Turner, William Blake, Charles Dickens, and George Eliot all made their names; or, in other fields in our own times, the singer Amy Winehouse and the actor Idris Elba.

Thomas Hardy (Dorset), John Constable (Suffolk), and Geoffrey Chaucer (Canterbury, Kent), from southern England contributed to the creative landscape, as did William Shakespeare (Stratford-upon-Avon) and Jane Austen (Bath). The Brontës (Yorkshire), the Beatles (Liverpool), and William Wordsworth (the Lake District) meanwhile did the same for northern England.

Scotland has given us the poet Robert Burns, writers James Barrie (*Peter Pan*), Robert Louis Stevenson (*Treasure Island*), and J. K. Rowling, author of the Harry Potter series. Other notable names include the architect and designer Charles Rennie Mackintosh from Glasgow, "the City of Architecture," as well as the '70s band the Bay City Rollers and, more recently, the singers Emeli Sandé and Lewis Capaldi.

The eighteenth-century Welsh painter Richard Wilson was a founding member of the Royal Academy, the Liberal Prime Minister David Lloyd George led Britain through the First World War, and Aneurin "Nye" Bevan inaugurated Britain's National Health Service (NHS) after the Second World War. The actors Catherine Zeta-Jones and Anthony Hopkins, the singers Bryn Terfel, Tom Jones, Katherine Jenkins, and Shirley Bassey, the poet Dylan Thomas, and the fashion designer Julien Macdonald are all part of the Welsh creative roll-call.

Northern Ireland meanwhile is the birthplace of the author C. S. Lewis, the singer/songwriter Van Morrison, the golfer Rory McIlroy, and the actors Kenneth Branagh and Liam Neeson. It also gave us Betty Williams and Mairead Corrigan, who were awarded the Nobel Peace Prize in 1976 for their efforts to end violent conflict during the Troubles.

THE MONARCHY

The monarchy is Britain's oldest institution of government. It dates back to Egbert, King of Wessex, who united England under his rule in 829 CE. The only interruption to it was the short-lived republic, or Commonwealth, established by Oliver Cromwell, which lasted between 1649 and 1660. This brief experiment with republicanism was mourned by few.

The Role of the Monarch

On the death of Queen Elizabeth II, the longest-reigning monarch, her eldest son, Charles, succeeded to the throne. The King's official title is "Charles the Third, by the Grace of God, of the United Kingdom of Great Britain and Northern Ireland and of his other Realms and Territories King, Head of the Commonwealth, Defender of the Faith."

Queen Elizabeth II on her Coronation Day, June 2, 1953, by Cecil Beaton (cropped).

THE BRITISH COMMONWEALTH OF NATIONS

TOGETHER

War Office poster produced in 1945.

In addition to being the UK's Head of State, the King is also Head of State of fourteen "Commonwealth realms." These are Antigua and Barbuda, Australia, the Bahamas, Belize, Canada, Grenada, Jamaica, New Zealand, Papua New Guinea, Saint Kitts and Nevis, Saint Lucia, Saint Vincent and the Grenadines, and the Solomon Islands, where he is represented by a Governor-General, appointed by him on advice from the ministers of the countries concerned and independent of the British government. He is also Head of State for Tuvalu in the South Pacific Ocean.

Some of these nations—notably Antigua and Barbuda, the Bahamas, Belize, Grenada, Jamaica, Saint Kitts and Nevis, Saint Lucia, Saint Vincent and the Grenadines, and Tuvalu—have expressed a desire to become a republic, as Barbados did in 2021.

Royal Assent

When a Bill has passed through all its stages in Parliament, it is sent to the King for Royal Assent, after which it becomes an Act of Parliament and becomes law. Over the centuries, the monarch's absolute power has been almost eliminated, and the King acts on the advice of his government ministers. He has a weekly meeting with the prime minister, receives accounts of cabinet decisions, and signs state papers.

In legal terms, the King is head of the executive and therefore Head of State; he is an integral part of the government's legislature; he is head of the judiciary and commander-in-chief of all the armed forces of the Crown. He is also "supreme governor" of the established Church, the Church of England.

GOVERNMENT AND POLITICS: A BIRD'S-EYE VIEW

While Britain is regarded as the "Cradle of Democracy," it is actually at odds with the rest of the developed world in that it does not have a written constitution, or, in other words, the UK has no single document that sets out the principles by which it is governed. Instead, laws and statutes are passed determining the nature of democracy and the freedoms enjoyed by the people as an ongoing process. Accordingly, legal justice is largely based on what is called the rule of precedent—thus previous legal judgments inform the present. This system is occasionally debated, for example, when the

Political and Constitutional Reform Select Committee of the House of Commons proposed a "new Magna Carta," which resulted in a consultation between Parliament and the people in 2015.

Britain's entire legal system, from its dress to its court conventions, is steeped in history, mostly dating back to the eighteenth and nineteenth centuries. Etiquette rules that members of parliament (MPs) do not use each other's names; colleagues are called "my honorable friend," whereas opponents are referred to as "the honorable gentleman (or lady)." There is no applause; MPs show agreement with shouts of "here, here."

It is fair to say that October 1, 2009 marked a defining moment in the UK's constitutional history as judicial authority was transferred from the House of Lords to a new Supreme Court in the historic setting of the former Middlesex Guildhall on Parliament Square. The Supreme Court is the final court of appeal in the UK for civil cases, and for criminal cases from England, Wales, and Northern Ireland. It hears cases of the greatest public or constitutional importance affecting the whole population.

If you are in London, it is well worth visiting the Public Gallery when the House of Commons is sitting in order to experience the "Mother of all Parliaments" firsthand.

England and Wales continue to have different legal, judicial, and local government systems from Scotland just as they did before the Act of Union (1707). They also have a different police force, national Church, and education systems. Since 1999, Scotland has had its own Scottish Parliament (Pàrlamaid na h-Alba), while Wales has had the National Assembly for Wales (now Senedd Cymru), with considerably fewer powers. Northern Ireland has also had its own self-government (the Northern Ireland Assembly), which was returned to it in 2007.

The World's Oldest Parliament

Interestingly, the world's oldest self-governing legislature is to be found in the Tynwald on the Isle of Man, which has been in continuous existence for more than a thousand years. Under the nominal sovereignty of Norway until 1266, it came under the direct administration of the British Crown in 1765. It has two branches, the Legislative Council and the House of Keys, which sit separately to consider legislation, but also sit together in the capital, Douglas, and annually at St. John's, for other parliamentary purposes.

Political Parties

General elections to vote in a new government take place every four or five years. Broadly speaking, the political system in Britain is divided along class lines, although all parties would protest that they are founded on ideological principles.

The Conservatives are also referred to as "Tories." Historically, the party saw itself as defending tradition,

The Houses of Parliament in Westminster. Victoria Tower is on the left, the Elizabeth Tower with "Big Ben" is on the right.

the landed gentry, and the middle classes; but in today's world it appeals across the cultural spectrum. Key policies include strengthening the economy, shrinking waiting lists to see a GP (doctor) or to have an operation, and reducing illegal immigration.

The Labour Party, founded at the end of the nineteenth century by the trade union movement, traditionally saw itself as the representative of the working classes. The former "Blairite" Labour Party (1997–2010), however, appealed, above all, to the middle class, which includes many "floating voters." But after losing the elections in 2010, it has reconnected with its traditional working-class supporters. As well as growing the economy and strengthening the NHS, it prioritizes clean energy, a reduction in crime, and childcare reform.

The third major party is the Liberal Democratic Party, formed in 1988 when the Liberal Party, which also has roots going back more than two hundred years, merged with the Social Democratic Party, formed in 1981. They occupy a position left of center. After the 2010 general elections, the Liberal Democrats formed a coalition government with the Conservatives until 2015, putting them back in office for the first time in more than seventy years. Its priorities include proportional representation, rejoining the EU, reducing household bills, and taxing water companies more to clean up Britain's waterways.

The Green Party won a seat in the House of Commons for the first time in 2010. As its name suggests, it fights for more insulated homes, reduced bus fares, and cleaner waterways. It also champions investment in social housing, a ban on no-fault evictions for renters, free school meals for schoolchildren, and thirty-five hours of free childcare. Growing concern over the climate crisis helped the party retain its seat in the 2015, 2017, and 2019 elections.

Scotland's largest political party—the center-left Scottish National Party (SNP)—gained 50 percent of the vote in Scotland in the 2015 elections. Its key policies are independence from the UK and rejoining the EU. It also campaigns to reduce poverty and ultimately to remove nuclear weapons from Scotland.

Like the SNP, Wales' center-left to left-wing party Plaid Cymru wants independence from the UK. It also fights for investment to be shared more equally, 100 percent renewable energy, and better-connected communities.

In the 2022 Northern Ireland elections Sinn Féin emerged as the largest party for the first time. Sinn Féin was established in 1905 with the goal of gaining Irish independence and unifying the island of Ireland. Today it also calls for social welfare reform, more affordable childcare, and a speedy transition to renewable energy.

The formerly dominant Democratic Unionist Party works toward a stronger economy, education, and healthcare system, and the removal of the Irish Sea trade border that was introduced between Northern Ireland and Britain in 2021 following the transition period after Britain voted to leave the EU.

Tory Rule

After thirteen years of Labour, the tide turned in the 2010 general elections. For the first time since 1974, no single party won the majority of votes, though the Conservatives won the most seats. This "hung parliament"—where no political party wins a majority— gave them two choices: form a minority government— which would require the support of MPs from other parties to pass legislation—or create a coalition government with another party. They chose the latter, and teamed up with the Liberal Democrats.

The Conservatives went on to win a majority in the 2015, 2017, and 2019 elections. Their stock fell after the Covid-19 pandemic and opponents criticized their high turnover of Tory prime ministers. The UK had five leaders in six years: David Cameron, Theresa May, Boris Johnson, and Liz Truss—who was in office for a record-breaking forty-four days—followed by Rishi Sunak.

KEY ISSUES

Austerity

Net borrowing, which is commonly referred to as "the deficit," is the difference between what the government spends and what it receives in taxes in a particular period. Since 1970–71, the government has had a surplus of funds in only five years, and the annual deficit has been around 3.7 percent of GDP.

When the Conservatives came to power, they promised to reduce the deficit by cutting public spending, which they said was necessary and unavoidable. This ushered in a new era of austerity. While borrowing increased after the 2007–08 financial crisis and the 2020–21 Covid-19 pandemic, overall the deficit is decreasing and is forecast to continue to do so.

The Cost of Living Crisis

The Conservatives' critics argue that their cuts have been too extreme, resulting in a fall in disposable income and a cost-of-living crisis. According to the Trussell Trust, a charity that alleviates hunger, food banks distributed more food parcels to those in need in 2022–23 than ever before—more than double than those donated in 2017–18.

The Housing Crisis

Not enough homes are being built to meet demand, so there is a shortage across Britain—particularly of apartments and houses to rent, social housing, and so-called "affordable housing," which has no legal definition. This has resulted in a housing crisis, with housebuilding in England at its lowest level since the Second World War.

The NHS Crisis

The publicly funded National Health Service was established in 1948 to provide free health care at the point of use for UK residents. Health care spending has increased in most years since because the population has grown, and because people are living longer with more complex health conditions. Despite this, funding in the decade before Covid-19 did not keep pace with demand—resulting in the NHS being unprepared for the pandemic, according to the British Medical Association. The result? Long waiting lists for patients, and low morale and pay for doctors—leading to junior doctors striking in 2022, 2023, and 2024, and senior doctors striking in 2023.

Terrorism

There are five threat levels in the UK—low, moderate, substantial, severe, and critical. This scale was made public a year after fifty-two people were killed by bombs on the Tube and a bus in London in 2005. Since then, major incidents have included the fatal shooting and stabbing of Labour MP Jo Cox in Leicestershire in 2016 and the stabbing of Conservative MP Sir David Amess in his constituency surgery in Essex in 2021. In recent years, five people were run over on Westminster Bridge, a police officer was stabbed to death in Parliament, twenty-two people were killed by a suicide bomber in

Manchester Arena, and eight people were run over and stabbed on London Bridge and in Borough Market. At the time of writing, the threat level was substantial, meaning an attack is likely.

However, it's not all doom and gloom. Britain is fighting back, and in 2023 the government launched a counter-terrorism strategy, Contest 2023. Its four pillars, prevent, pursue, protect, and prepare, are designed to intercept and mitigate terrorist attacks, so Britons can continue to go about their daily lives.

Brexit

The UK Independence Party (UKIP), now Reform UK, believed that Britain should leave the EU and limit immigration. This view appeared to be reflected in the result of the 2016 referendum on the UK's membership of the EU, which saw 51.9 percent vote to leave the EU and 48.1 percent choose to remain. The tight result reflected a divided Britain—and has been a matter of debate ever since.

COVID-19

The first known patients of Coronavirus, or Covid-19, were identified on December 21, 2019, in Wuhan, China. Ten days later, the Chinese authorities informed the World Health Organization that patients were suffering from "pneumonia of an unknown cause." Britain recorded its first confirmed cases on January 29, 2020. By that March, cases had surged. A nationwide lockdown was imposed on March 26, which meant Britons could only leave their homes for essential reasons, such as to buy food, until the rules were relaxed on May 10. A second national lockdown was announced in November, followed by a third in January 2021. All restrictions ended on February 24, 2022. The UK government was criticized for being slow to react to the crisis and for buying so much unusable personal protective equipment and praised for its vaccine research and prompt vaccine administration.

THE ECONOMY

Until the international banking crisis triggered a world recession in 2009, the economy had been one of the success stories of the New Labour administration (1997–2010). Britain had maintained low inflation and the lowest interest rates in a generation, achieving annual growth of around 2.5 percent—against a backdrop of a boom in the service and knowledge-based sectors but a depressed manufacturing base—as well as maintaining an independent currency. At the same time, the government levied the largest increases in indirect taxation in a generation to fund an increase in spending on public services, especially the NHS. After the 2010 elections, the Conservative–Lib Dem coalition introduced cuts to reduce the budget deficit.

The 2016 Brexit vote shook the economy, having a particularly negative impact on goods exports, with smaller firms being most affected. However, while the trade in goods was weakened, trade in services remained strong, according to the Office of National Statistics. The Centre for Economic Policy Research has found that business investment has also been low since 2016, with data and survey evidence suggesting that leaving the EU is partly responsible.

At the time of writing, inflation is high but coming down, with households and businesses adjusting to higher prices and interest rates by curbing consumption and investment. The economy is expected to escape a recession thanks to a better outlook for energy prices, a more resilient global environment, and a strong labor market. However, growth is expected to remain weak.

In terms of scientific research, Britain has become a leading world player. Recent high-profile examples include the creation of next-generation genome sequencing to increase the speed and reduce the cost of reading DNA, the launch of the James Webb Telescope—an international collaboration that has vastly expanded our knowledge of the universe—and a successful womb transplant from a living donor. Britain's share of Nobel Prizes is second only to that of the US in absolute terms, but is twice as many per capita.

Trading with the rest of world has always been the key to British economic prosperity. Until the Second World War Britain's principal trading partner was its Empire. In the 1980s, Prime Minister Margaret Thatcher was the first to warn that the loss of Britain's former captive markets obliged it to become more competitive. This occurred slowly and to some extent reluctantly, and British trade is not as strong as it was.

In the 1970s, '80s, and '90s, Britain was among the world's top five trading nations, after the USA, Germany, Japan, and France. That changed at the beginning of the twenty-first century, in part because of China's growing economy. Other developing countries also pushed Britain down the board, and in 2020 it sat in twelfth place, according to the United Nations Conference on Trade and Development.

Post-Brexit, Britain's principal trading partner for exported goods is the USA, followed by the Netherlands, Germany, Ireland, and France. Britain's main commodities are mechanical appliances followed by mineral fuels, motor vehicles, precious metals, and pharmaceutical products.

It is ironic that four of the ten most productive car plants in Europe are in Britain but foreign owned—Honda, Toyota, Nissan, and Vauxhall Motors (GM). Britain still manufactures many of the world's premium and sports marques, including Aston Martin, Bentley, Jaguar, Lotus, MG, and Rolls-Royce, demonstrating that the British worker can indeed be one of the best, given the right working environment and motivation.

It's not surprising that Britain's biggest foreign investor is the United States, and vice versa, since the two countries have a common history, language, and culture. It is important to recognize, however, that there are significant differences between them in the perception of history, the use of language, and in cultural norms and aspirations. This is not the place to examine these in detail, but it is useful for American visitors, especially businesspeople, to be aware of them.

CHAPTER TWO

SCOTLAND, WALES, & NORTHERN IRELAND

While Scotland, Wales, and Northern Ireland share some similarities with their larger neighbor, England, there are fundamental cultural differences. So, when visiting these countries, a degree of sensitivity and an awareness of their different histories and distinguishing national characteristics will always be appreciated and will certainly contribute to a more rewarding experience.

INTRODUCING SCOTLAND

The Scottish Highlands and Islands contain some of the world's most spectacular scenery. Britain's highest mountain, Ben Nevis (4,409 feet, 1,344 m) is in the Grampian Mountains. Scotland accounts for approximately a third of Britain's land mass but contains only 8 percent of the population

(5.4 million). Its population is slowly increasing, largely due to immigration, and a further 5 million people in the United States claim Scottish ancestry.

Scotland's two largest cities are Edinburgh (the capital, population 477,000 in 2011) on the east coast, and Glasgow (593,000) on the west coast; the two other principal cities are Aberdeen and Dundee. Scotland's islands are its least densely populated areas—the most populated of these are the Shetland Islands (23,000), the Orkney Islands (21,000), and Lewis and Harris (21,000). In all, of Scotland's total population, 104,000 people are islanders.

One of the most famous places in Scotland is Loch Ness, Britain's largest body of fresh water, which is allegedly home to a "monster" called "Nessie" that has captured the world's imagination since the first "sighting" by John and Aldie Mackay in 1933. Loch Ness is a major tourist attraction, and its secrets will no doubt continue to engage the worlds of science, literature, and Hollywood for years to come. At the time of writing, no monster has been found.

The next most famous place is probably the eight-hundred-year-old Edinburgh Castle. There have been strategic buildings and royal residences on top of the striking volcanic Castle Rock since the eleventh century, when it was home to Margaret, wife of King Malcolm III. It was later used as a military garrison and prison. The sheer rock face and scale dominate Edinburgh's skyline and can be seen from every direction as you approach the city. The Edinburgh Tattoo, held annually in August over a three-week

Edinburgh's ancient castle, which has played a prominent role in Scottish history.

period and featuring massed pipe bands, is the principal annual event to be held at the castle, concluding with a spectacular fireworks display, an event enjoyed by millions on TV across the globe.

HISTORICAL PERSPECTIVES

The relationship between England and Scotland has been somewhat strained for centuries. In 1297, during the First War of Scottish Independence, Sir William Wallace inflicted the first defeat of English forces in the Battle of Stirling Bridge—he was later executed in London.

Nearly forty years later, in 1314, Robert the Bruce defeated the English once more, this time at the Battle of Bannockburn, near Stirling—effectively putting an end to the attempts of the English King Edward I to annex Scotland and impose English rule. This resulted in Edward III's formal recognition in 1328 of Robert the Bruce as Robert I of Scotland.

The Scottish and English monarchies united in 1603, with the first "union" king, James I, using the title "King of Great Britain" to signify the confederation. However, during the English Civil War (1642–6), the Scots supported the Parliamentarians—who were also known as the Roundheads, because of the shape of their helmets—during their fight against the Royalists, who wanted Charles I to retain his absolute powers.

The Parliamentarians won, although the Scots went on to suffer a brief occupation under the Parliamentarian Oliver Cromwell's Commonwealth because of Presbyterian–Royalist uprisings in 1648.

The 1707 Act of Union was another turning point, which saw the English and Scottish Parliaments merge into a single Parliament based at Westminster— creating the new state of Britain. The Union Flag was a combination of the two national flags—the red cross of St. George and the blue diagonal cross of St. Andrew, also known as the Saltire.

Following the Act of Union, there were more uprisings. Charles Edward Stuart, or "Bonnie Prince Charlie," led the most famous of these, and after some success was finally defeated in 1746 at Culloden, near Inverness, in the Scottish Highlands.

GAELIC

Scottish Gaelic is a Celtic language, akin to Irish. As a spoken language it is being actively supported by the Scottish Parliament (Pàrlamaid na h-Alba), with 58,000 speakers who are competent enough to use it as a first language. The 2005 Gaelic Language Act seeks to "accord equal status" to English and Gaelic. Today, just over half (51.5 percent) of all Gaelic speakers in Scotland live in Eilean Siar, known as the Western Isles, Highlands, and Argyll and Bute in the western Highlands. The main institution for Gaelic culture is the An Communn Gàidhealach, in Inverness.

CULTURAL SYMBOLS

Clans and Tartans

Scottish life and culture used to be split between the cities, towns, and villages of the Lowlands, or Borders, where intellectual, scientific, and literary life was nurtured, and the Highlands, where social life revolved around the clan system, *clann* in Gaelic meaning children or family. Loyalty was paramount for survival since the clan chief was a leader, protector, and dispenser of justice at gallow hills and beheading pits, which can still be seen today. Kinship ties created a powerful social unit. Clan feuds, popularized by Sir Walter Scott in his novel *Rob Roy*, were commonplace and frequently deadly. The Scottish monarchs tended to leave the Highlands well alone.

Cèilidh dance competion at the Highland Games.

After the final crushing defeat of the Scots at the Battle of Culloden in 1746, the 1747 Act of Proscription introduced sweeping changes to the Highland way of life. These outlawed wearing tartan, including kilts, teaching Gaelic, and carrying arms. In addition, heritable (clan) jurisdictions were abolished and even bagpipes could not be played in public. In fact, anything to do with Highland life was deemed undesirable. From the late 1700s to the mid-1800s, many Scots were forcibly evicted from their homes to make way for sheep farms, in an act dubbed the Highland Clearances. This, along with the resulting mass exodus of Scots to North America, Australia, and New Zealand, almost destroyed Highland culture.

However, in 1782 the Act of Proscription was repealed, which led to the commercialization and standardization of tartans, with the first tartan pattern books becoming available shortly after. Historians note that George IV wore a tartan on his visit to Scotland in 1822, which gave rise to a nineteenth-century tartan boom, nurtured by Queen Victoria, who had a special fondness for the Highlands. Her personal servant (and in later life companion) John Brown was from Aberdeenshire.

Today, a tartan exists for every occasion, whether it be for everyday wear, hunting, or formal dress. Given the advances in the weaving and dyeing industry, it is not surprising that tartan links to the historic clans have become increasingly stretched, giving rise to the more than 2,500 tartans and variations now controlled by the official government Scottish Register of Tartans (www.tartanregister.gov.uk).

Bagpipes

Although known to the Egyptians and Romans millennia ago, there is no doubt that today the "sound" of Scotland is the bagpipes. The earliest piping competitions took place at the annual Falkirk Tryst in 1781, when Highlanders were penalized for wearing kilts or playing the "warlike" instrument, as the English considered it.

There is no sound on earth so stirring and elemental as that of massed pipes. The band of the Queen's Own Cameron Highlanders and others can be heard daily at Edinburgh Castle during the Edinburgh Tattoo in August, and at other major public occasions such as Highland Gatherings (games), most famously the Cowal Highland Gathering (Cowal Games) held in Dunoon every August. The games invariably include pipe concerts and competitions. In the past, most clan chiefs boasted a personal piper—a tradition that gave rise to legendary piping families, such as the MacCrimmons, MacLeods, and MacArthurs. Towns, police departments, and Highland regiments have pipe bands—among the most famous is the Shotts and Dykehead Caledonia Pipe Band.

Golf

Golf—widely recognized as one of the world's oldest, most sophisticated, and most prestigious sports— has come a long way since the ancient game of *gowff*, which involved whacking a stone with a stick. The earliest mention of golf as a game that we would recognize goes back to 1457, when its popularity was so great that it (along with "futeball") had to be prohibited on Sundays because it interfered with archery practice. In 1754 a society of golfers was formed in the university city of St. Andrews. In 1834, under the patronage of William IV, this became the Royal and Ancient Golf Club of St. Andrews, and the ruling body of the game in Britain.

Food and Drink

Oats have long dominated the Scottish diet. "Tatties and herring," potatoes with herring in oatmeal, is a typical main meal. The popularity of oats lives on today in porridge, oatcakes, and flapjacks.

A Burns Supper: haggis, neeps (diced or mashed swedes/turnips), and tatties (potatoes).

Since the mid-1800s, Scots have started the day with a traditional Scottish breakfast, which might include fried eggs, tomatoes, mushrooms, and tattie scones (potato patties) alongside bacon, black pudding (blood sausage), and haggis.

Haggis, the national dish, is also traditionally enjoyed on Burns Night on January 25, which celebrates the poet Robert Burns' birthday. It consists of chopped offal mixed with suet, oatmeal, onions, and herbs, and boiled in a sheep's stomach. It's eaten with mashed potatoes and turnips, and nowadays there is even a vegetarian version. Other favorites include beef, venison, and smoked fish such as Arbroath smokies (smoked haddock) and Scottish smoked salmon.

As for dessert, Scots are partial to shortbread, fruity Dundee cake, and cranachan, a creamy sweet made with honey, raspberries, oatmeal, and whisky or Drambuie. Oats and whisky feature in Atholl brose, too—a kind of cranachan in liquid form.

In Britain, whiskey is spelled "whisky." Scotland has more than a hundred distilleries, most of which are in the northeast, and in 2022 global exports rocketed to £6 billion, according to the Scotch Whisky Association. Malt whisky, in particular, is distilled according to age-old methods and is relished around the world.

There are more than one hundred classified single malts, divided into five regions: the Highlands, Lowlands, isle of Islay, Campeltown, and Speyside. The distilleries on Islay, and in Speyside and the Highlands are particularly well known. Familiar names include Cardhu and Dallas Dhu—established in 1899 and now run by Historic Buildings and Monuments—as well as Glen Grant, Glenfarclas, Glenfiddich, The Glenlivet, Glenmorangie, Linkwood, The Macallan, Mortlach, Strathisla, Tamdhu, and Tamnavulin.

Blended whiskies are the most common worldwide, but malt whisky consumption is growing as drinkers discover its subtleties. Has the water that goes into the making of the malt, for example, been filtered through peat or over granite? Is the shape of the still significant? Has the barley been home grown or imported? Connoisseurs will tell you it's all "in the "nose." The Scotch Whisky Heritage Centre in Edinburgh provides a comprehensive introduction to the whisky industry.

Whisky wasn't always Scotland's top tipple. In the seventeenth and eighteenth centuries the favored drink was claret, shipped in from Bordeaux to Leith. Indeed, Robert Burns testified to the vast quantities that were consumed in his song "The Silver Tassie" in the line, "Gae bring tae me a point o'wine." The tax on wine put an end to its popularity, and gave the cue for the old illegal stills to go public (and legal) and develop the high-value-added whisky industry that exists today.

THE SCOTTISH ECONOMY

When it comes to financial services, Scotland excels: its leading industry, which includes cyber security, is valued at £17.4 billion. Global business services, such as call centers, are also a prized sector, employing 230,000 people and earning £15 billion—in part because Scottish accents are considered to be professional, reassuring, and engaging.

Technology is significant too. Around 100,000 work in the digital field, from engineering software to wireless communication—making it worth £6.5 billion.

Despite the climate crisis, the oil and gas industries are still creating around 168,750 jobs, and contribute £9.2 billion to the economy, although renewable energy is a growing sector.

Tourism, aerospace, and the creative industries—which include gaming, animation, music, and the arts—each bring in around £4 billion.

Scotland is home to one of Europe's largest life science clusters, with 771 life science companies. Pioneering scientific breakthroughs include the cloning of Dolly the sheep, the development of MRI scanners, and the discovery of the p53 cancer-suppressor gene. Much of this technology is created in "Silicon Glen," in the corridor between Glasgow and Edinburgh.

INTRODUCING WALES

In its native language, Wales is known as *Cymru*, which roughly translates as "the country of friends." In English it is known simply as Wales—a land of chapels and farms amid valleys and vast, mountainous spaces. It is the land where there is a growing passion to speak the Welsh language and consequently where, uniquely in Britain, most official signs and documents are bilingual.

Wales is also the land of the male voice choir— which has its origins in the old coal mines and iron foundries. Among the most famous contemporary Welsh choirs are the Dunvant, Morriston Orpheus, Pendyrus, Treorchy, and the Welsh National Opera. In common with the other Celtic cultures of Scotland and Ireland, the Welsh love theater, poetry, oratory, debate, and storytelling, and are well represented among the great names, past and present.

Not surprisingly, given the ethereal beauty of its geography and ever-changing climate, sitting as it does as Britain's front door to the prevailing Atlantic weather systems, Wales is a source of inspiration to writers, musicians, artists, and craftspeople around the world. All this is encapsulated in the National Eisteddfod of Wales, the largest annual music and poetry competition in Europe, where lyrical poetry is sung to a harp accompaniment and male voice choirs go for gold.

THE PEOPLE AND THE LANGUAGE

The population of Wales is just over three million, with more than half living in the industrialized south. Cardiff is the largest city (population 362,000 in 2021), followed by Swansea (238,000 in 2021).

The Welsh language is spoken widely—although this is not so evident in the capital, Cardiff. In 2022, an annual population survey found that 29.5 percent of the population are Welsh speakers, with Welsh being the first language spoken in the rural north and west of the country. As noted, it also appears on all road signs, public notices, and official buildings. Apart from some isolated areas where Welsh is the first language, everyone also speaks English, and BBC Cymru Wales broadcasts in English and Welsh. According to the 2011 census, the percentage of the population who can speak Welsh dropped from 21 percent in 2001 to 19 percent. Gwynedd is the only region where more than half the population speaks, reads, and writes Welsh. Since 2000 Welsh has been taught as a first or second language to pupils throughout Wales. Proposals to increase Welsh-language teaching in Wales is an ongoing controversial subject. The Welsh language is full of consonants and has a unique, undulating rhythm, which has transferred to the accent of the Welsh when speaking English.

Aspects of local life, traditionally informed by a strict chapel Methodism, can feel parochial, and the people are not especially enthusiastic about the English. But that shouldn't deter you from enjoying its rich Celtic culture and traditions.

GEOGRAPHY AND HISTORY

The most famous of the Welsh highland areas is
Snowdonia National Park in the north of the country,
which spreads across 825 square miles (2,137 sq. km).
Snowdon (*Yr Wyddfa*), its highest peak, rises to 3,560 feet
(1,085 m). Although the north is the most mountainous
area, central Wales has some beautiful hills. The Severn,
at 210 miles (338 km), is Britain's longest river. The
Brecon Beacons are the center of another National Park
of about 500 square miles (1,300 sq. km). The Welsh
mountains are important sources of water for Wales, and
for English cities such as Liverpool and Birmingham.

View of a mountain lake in Snowdonia National Park.

Long before the Romans left Britain, Wales was an autonomous Celtic stronghold ruled by sovereign princes. In the eleventh century, the emerging Anglo-Norman kingdom of England found it increasingly difficult to maintain law and order along its borders resulting from the rivalry rife among the Welsh princes. William the Conqueror attempted to find a solution, without much success, to the "Welsh problem." In the second half of the twelfth century, Henry II set up "divide and rule" schemes where his Anglo-Norman Marcher barons ruthlessly governed small jurisdictions such as Chepstow, Brecon, and Monmouth, and the Marches border areas between England, Wales, and Scotland.

Stainless steel statue of Llywelyn ap Gruffydd Fychan overlooking the town of Llandovery.

Matters came to a head in 1282 when the king, Edward I, through his Marcher barons, brought Wales under English rule by defeating the last native Welsh prince, Llywelyn ap Gruffydd, at the battle of Orewin Bridge in mid-Wales. This signaled the end of any hope of an independent country. Edward consolidated his position by commissioning the Savoyard architect Master James of St. George to build a series of magnificent, impregnable castles, including Aberystwyth, Caernarvon, Conway, Flint, and Harlech, in strategic positions across Wales. The building project was breathtaking, on a scale likened to Hadrian's Wall, constructed during the Emperor Hadrian's rule in around 122 CE. Nothing greater has taken place in Britain since.

To consolidate his power further, Edward I's son, later Edward II, was born in Caernarvon Castle in

1284 and declared the first English Prince of Wales. The eldest son of the reigning monarch still bears this title; King Charles was made Prince of Wales in 1969, his son Prince William in 2022.

By the turn of the fifteenth century, Welsh resentment over English laws and administration, together with widespread poverty and economic hardship, brought the nationalist leader Owain Glyndwr (Owen Glendower) into open confrontation with King Henry IV. After some initial success against the English, Glyndwr was defeated by Henry and the Prince of Wales at the Battle of Shrewsbury in 1403. The Welsh may have been defeated, but before the century was out, blood ties linked them inextricably to the English monarchy.

Visionary head of Owen Glendower by William Blake, 1819.

With the accession of Henry VII in 1485, the Tudor dynasty came into being, bringing with it important Welsh ancestry. As a result, under Henry VIII, two key Acts of Union in 1536 and 1542 united England and Wales administratively, politically, and legally. This has remained the case until the present day; hence you will see references to the laws "governing England and Wales," while Scotland and Northern Ireland have their own legislatures and legal systems.

A referendum was held in Wales in 1997, as part of the then Labour government's policy of devolution, to decide whether Wales should have an independent Assembly with some control over Welsh affairs (the National Assembly for Wales). The referendum attracted about a third of the electorate, with those in favor coming barely ahead of those who rejected the idea. Nevertheless, it may be seen in years to come as a turning point in Welsh history. The Assembly is responsible for education, health, business, culture, and sports. Westminster continues to control foreign affairs, defense, taxation, overall economic policy, crime, justice, prisons, social security, and broadcasting.

THE WELSH ECONOMY

In the eighteenth and nineteenth centuries, the Industrial Revolution had a major impact in south Wales, where iron and steel factories and coal mines were concentrated. Cardiff grew in the nineteenth century as a coal exporting port, and Swansea and Newport's prosperity also depended on coal, iron, and steel, as well as their position as ports in the Bristol Channel. Merthyr Tydfil and Ebbw Vale were among the most famous steel towns. Over time, of course, all the valleys where coal was accessible attracted settlers.

The coal was transported to the ports by railways and canals—most famously, the Monmouthshire canal to Newport, which opened in 1791.

The arrival of the Sony UK Technology Center in 1992 in Mid Glamorgan was a historic moment. It is the only center outside Japan to produce high-definition camera units. Today there are several significant areas of high-end manufacturing in Wales.

Wales is home to a hundred and sixty aerospace and defense companies employing 20,000 people. Some of the world's biggest companies in the field have bases in Wales, including Airbus, BAE Systems, and GE Aviation. The Airbus wing manufacturing center in Broughton meanwhile is the UK's biggest aerospace manufacturing operation.

Wales also employs 13,000 people in the automotive sector, which generates £2.6 billion sales annually. It's home to thirty "Tier 1" suppliers, including Ford and Toyota.

The country has particular expertise in alternative fuels such as hydrogen and is a leading UK region for developing a low-carbon infrastructure for vehicles in collaboration with Welsh academic centers of excellence.

Wales also specializes in optoelectronics, or, in other words, the development of electronic devices and systems that detect and control visible light and invisible forms of radiation such as gamma rays, X-rays, and ultraviolet and infrared light. It's strong in communications, sensors, and lasers as well.

CULTURAL SYMBOLS

Daffodils
Daffodils are culturally significant to the Welsh as they are associated with Saint David's Day on March 1. St. David is the patron saint of Wales. A common sight in gardens, these vibrant yellow flowers symbolize rebirth and the coming of spring. They were adopted by Welsh regiments in the nineteenth century and are worn as a symbol of national pride during celebrations.

Welsh Love Spoons
A traditional love token given by young men to their sweethearts, Welsh love spoons are hand-carved from a single piece of wood and decorated with intricate heart, bell, or lock motifs. They are often exchanged

Carved Welsh love spoon.

Welsh flag on a building in Cardiff.

between couples or on special occasions to express love and commitment, and are displayed in homes.

The Welsh Dragon

The Welsh red dragon, Y Ddraig Goch, is a heraldic symbol that has represented Wales since the early Tudor period. Linked to ancient mythology, it embodies Welsh identity and resistance. The emblem graces the Welsh flag as well as numerous landmarks such as Cardiff Castle.

INTRODUCING NORTHERN IRELAND

Geographically, Northern Ireland is part of the island of Ireland, although at its closest point it is separated from Scotland by a mere 13 miles (21 km) of water, the North Channel. It consists of six counties: Antrim, Armagh, Down, Fermanagh, Derry/Londonderry, and Tyrone. Northern Ireland is often called Ulster, even though it includes only six of the nine counties of the former province of Ulster.

After a bitter war of independence, the Anglo-Irish Treaty of 1921 offered the people of Ireland a choice between self-governing "dominion" status or remaining part of Britain. Twenty-six predominantly Catholic counties, including three from Ulster, chose independence as a republic, leaving only the six northern, and in those days largely Protestant, counties of Ulster to remain part of and loyal to Britain. For this reason they call themselves Loyalists (or Unionists).

Thus, Northern Ireland is largely divided between the Protestant descendants of those English and Scottish settlers who consider themselves British, and Catholics who identify as Irish. This results in occasional conflicts, so it is advisable to avoid taboo topics such as religion and politics in conversation. But generally security is not a problem and visitors receive a warm welcome across Northern Ireland.

The Peace Bridge over the Foyle River in Derry.

HISTORICAL PERSPECTIVES

Archaeological evidence suggests a brief Roman occupation two thousand years ago. English history in Ireland goes back to the time of Henry II (1154–89), who in 1171 landed at Waterford with four thousand men and the blessing of Pope Adrian IV. Within weeks he had ensured that all the Irish bishops acknowledged the authority of Rome, and most of the Gaelic kings paid him homage.

In the generations that followed, a new feudal Ireland emerged, based on the Norman–English model, complete with castles, manors, walled towns, and monasteries.

In 1605, Catholics were blamed for the failed attempt to assassinate King James I in Parliament in what is known as the Gunpowder Plot. This gave rise to anti-

Mural of William III ("King Billy") in Shankill Parade, Belfast.

Catholic Penal Laws, and in 1607 King James confiscated land to create "plantations," then encouraged Protestants from England and Scotland to settle on them in Ulster.

One of the most famous of these plantations was Derry, renamed Londonderry when areas of the city were given to City of London livery companies for development. They constructed walls around the city, built a town hall, an Anglican cathedral, stately streets, and homes to attract a new Protestant upper class to govern the indigenous Catholic population. Unsurprisingly, much of the tortured modern history of Ireland has its roots in this so-called "Plantation" period.

In 1641, just before the English Civil War, the Catholic Irish rebelled. They eventually sided with the Royalists and were savagely suppressed by Oliver Cromwell, leader of the Parliamentary forces, whose name is loathed in the south.

After the English forced James II (1685–88), the last Stuart king, who had converted to Catholicism, to abandon the throne, he fled to France where he organized an army and attempted a comeback. On July 12, 1690, the new Protestant king, William of Orange, defeated the Catholic French and Irish forces under James at the Battle of the Boyne. King Billy (as he was popularly known) and his white horse can still be seen painted on the sides of many Belfast end-of-terrace houses.

In 1791, inspired by the American and French Revolutions and seeking to turn Ireland into an independent republic, a group of radical reformers established the Society of United Irishmen. The French subsequently sent a fleet of thirty-five ships to Bantry Bay to help them, but the plan failed owing to bad weather. The movement was suppressed after a failed rebellion in 1798. The Act of Union of 1800 abolished the Irish Parliament, and Ireland was incorporated into the United Kingdom of Great Britain and Ireland in 1801.

William Pitt, the English prime minister, promised various political concessions to the Catholics as part of the Union deal. But in the end, George III refused to sanction them, saying that it would cause him to be disloyal to his coronation oath to defend the Protestant religion if he did so. Pitt resigned in protest.

THE POLITICAL LANDSCAPE

Northern Ireland has a 224-mile (360-km) border with the Irish Republic, forming the UK's only land boundary with a member state of the EU. About half the 1.8 million population live in the eastern coastal region, at the center of which is the capital, Belfast (population just under 300,000). Other major towns include Lisburn, Derry/Londonderry, Omagh, Antrim, and Bangor. There are twenty-six local government district councils and eighteen members of Parliament elected to the House of Commons in Westminster.

Planting Scottish Protestant settlers with a Presbyterian culture among the indigenous Catholic population was always going to be problematic. Mounting tensions resulted in thirty years of conflict from the late 1960s to the late 1990s, an era known as "The Troubles." The 1998 Good Friday Agreement largely resolved the conflict as it introduced a power-sharing agreement between Protestants and Catholics. The UK government agreed to devolve, or share, some of its powers by means of the Northern Ireland Act 1998, which led to the establishment of a Northern Ireland Assembly, which makes laws for Northern Ireland, and a Northern Ireland Executive, which implements the laws and runs Northern Ireland on a day-to-day basis.

The Northern Ireland Assembly sits in the Parliament Building at Stormont, in Belfast, and its 108 members have full legislative and executive powers.

However, in 2002, it was suspended following a failure to reach a consensus on aspects of the peace process, including the contentious issue of arms decommissioning. There have been several suspensions and reinstatements, the last over differences arising from the post-Brexit trade barrier down the Irish Sea. Following elections in 2022, in

The Northern Ireland Parliament buildings at Stormont, Belfast.

which the Irish nationalist party Sinn Féin emerged as the largest party, followed by the Democratic Unionist Party, devolved government was restored.

Reunion with the Republic of Ireland continues to be an ideal for many Catholics in the North, and is the stated political objective of Sinn Féin. The 2021 census showed that 45.7 percent of people in Northern Ireland identify as Catholic, compared to 43.5 percent Protestants.

The most visibly challenging cultural aspect of the two traditions is the so-called marching season, which runs from Easter to the end of September, and is essentially the preserve of the Protestant community. The biggest parades in July mark the victory of William III over James II at the Battle of the Boyne. Such parades tend to be triumphalist in nature, featuring banners and bands. They are mostly organized by Protestant/Unionist associations, including "Orangemen," who took their name from King William's family, the Dutch House of Orange. There is a Parades Commission that endeavors to strike a balance regarding the time and place for parades.

CULTURAL SYMBOLS

Green

Dubbed the "Emerald Isle" because of its rolling hills and meadows, Ireland has long been associated with the color green. The color is also a symbol for Roman Catholics, hence the Republic of Ireland's tricolor flag, which depicts white—a symbol of peace—between green and Protestant orange.

The shamrock is another visible manifestation of the Catholic community's connection with green. Tradition holds that St. Patrick, Ireland's Romano-British-born patron saint, used the clover's three petals to illustrate the doctrine of the Holy Trinity. Local Catholics wear shamrocks with pride every St. Patrick's Day (March 17). A public holiday in Northern Ireland, St. Patrick's Day is celebrated by Catholics and a growing number of Protestants, particularly at an annual parade in Belfast.

The Harp

The Irish have been playing the harp since medieval times, and it has found its way into folklore, poetry, and literature. In the 1700s

Wooden Irish harp.

and 1800s, Irish Nationalists adopted the emblem as a symbol of resistance against British rule, and in 1862 it was added to the label of Guinness beer. Today the harp is played at national events and Irish dance performances.

The Leprechaun

The mischievous elf of Irish folklore is commonly depicted in a green hat and coat, with a flame-colored beard and hair. According to legend, he lives alone in a cave or forest and hides a pot of gold at the end of a rainbow.

The Red Hand of Ulster

The Red Hand of Ulster, often seen on flags and murals, is thought to originate in a grim legend about two chiefs racing across a stretch of water in a bid to be the first to reach Ulster and claim rights to the land. Realizing his opponent was in the lead, one chieftain cut off his hand and threw it onto the shore. The emblem is common to both communities. To Protestants it represents Northern Ireland's six counties, while to Catholics it represents the original nine counties of Ulster, three of which are in the Republic of Ireland.

Londonderry's coat of arms.

Flax

The flax plant has been cultivated on the island of Ireland since the eleventh century, as its fibers are used to weave linen. In the nineteenth century, flax farming and linen manufacturing formed a significant part of the local economy, and Belfast in particular was known for producing good-quality linen. The Northern Ireland Assembly's logo features the flax plant's pale blue blossom to signify Northern Ireland's six counties.

The Acorn

County Derry is one of the nine historical counties of Ulster and one of the six counties that make up Northern Ireland. Derry is an anglicization of the Irish word *doire*, which means oak grove or oak wood, hence the area's nickname—the oak leaf county. Rooted in Celtic heritage, the acorn symbolizes growth, strength, and resilience in Derry/Londonderry. Visitors will see the motif on buildings, in local art, and at cultural events.

THE NORTHERN IRISH ECONOMY

Northern Ireland's linen industry had declined by the 1950s, linen having been replaced by cotton and manmade fibers. Agriculture and shipbuilding—led by Harland & Wolff in Belfast—also began to decline in the face of Asian competition and a rise in air travel.

However, after a challenging few decades, the 2007–08 global recession and Covid-19 lockdowns, Northern Ireland's economy has not only largely recovered but also grown, with unemployment dropping in 2023.

Engineering and manufacture, which includes aerospace, electronics, and renewable energy, is a developing sector, accounting for 15 percent of output and 11 percent of jobs—with 12,000 people working in sustainable energy alone.

The service industry is also strong, with 40,000 people employed in financial services, 20,000 people working in global business services, and 18,000 in the legal and management sector.

Construction accounts for 14 percent of output, making it Northern Ireland's third-largest industry, although in 2023 it took a dip along with the production of textiles, tobacco, food, and drink. Food security and traceability, however, is a strength: Northern Ireland created the electronic cattle-tracing database APHIS and helped develop Food Fortress, a collaboration of businesses committed to food security.

That's in part because of Northern Ireland's gains in technology, which include areas such as cyber security, artificial intelligence, and telecoms—resulting in the *Financial Times* identifying Belfast as one of the world's top 15 digital economies of the future in 2021.

Creative technology, such as animation, gaming, film, and TV, is also performing well, as indicated by the filming of the hit fantasy drama *Game of Thrones* across Northern Ireland and the post-production house Yellowmoon's Oscar, Emmy, and BAFTA nominations.

Life sciences, cruise tourism, retail, and motor vehicle repair services are also significant contributors.

CHAPTER THREE

VALUES &
ATTITUDES

Given Britain's varied ethnicities, classes, and religious beliefs, you might well conclude that there isn't such a thing as a uniform "British culture." The English, however, are by far the largest group within the British Isles and are therefore culturally dominant.

FAIR PLAY

Tolerance, fair play, and an instinct for compromise are fundamental British qualities, along with a strong sense of justice. Hence the existence of a centuries-old legal system, the extensive volunteer and charity network, and a national acceptance of standing in line—people patiently waited for 24 hours in a 10-mile (16 km) queue to file past Queen Elizabeth II's coffin as she lay in state in Westminster Hall in the Palace of Westminster in September 2022.

In more recent times, however, the consensus has shifted from a sense of obligation to a new focus on individual rights and self-interest, and the traditional concern for fairness that informed behavior is less apparent. In turn, this attitude has fed into "single issue" politics, which tend to engage in extremes, such as the animal rights movement or the ultra-right-wing British National Party. The British are also becoming a more litigious people.

MODESTY AND UNDERSTATEMENT

Whether it's a matter of style or a deeper sense of propriety, by and large British people do not blow their own trumpet. The wealthy tend to live discreetly, away from the public gaze, and high-flyers do not generally brag about their accomplishments. As the saying goes, "Self-praise is no recommendation." The English are masters of the art of understatement, which may or may not be intentionally amusing. Self-deprecation—a seeming disparagement of oneself—is a trait not always understood by foreigners. Making light of failure or awkward moments and being overly humble about an achievement is standard, as in "I can barely run a bath, let alone a race."

A certain sense of decorum and not wishing to "make a scene" can lead to putting up with a bad situation without complaining, and even to a degree of social hypocrisy. It's not unknown for people to grumble about an indifferent meal in a restaurant, only to tell the waiter how delicious it was at the end of it.

People filing quietly past Queen Elizabeth's coffin in Westminster Hall.

Quite distinct from the desire to avoid socially awkward moments is the famous British "stiff upper lip." This expression refers to British stoicism, the ability to remain resolute and unemotional when faced with adversity, an attribute celebrated in Rudyard Kipling's poem "If." Thus a British person might describe a challenging situation as "a bit tricky," and if you were to ask someone how they are, expect a generic "I'm fine, thanks" in response, even if they've just lost their job, dog, or parent—all in the spirit of "Mustn't grumble."

HUMOR

Humor punctuates daily life, thanks to the British ability to poke fun at themselves—depicted in sketch shows such as "Yes Minister," "Monty Python," and "Little Britain."

Wild understatements such as "It's a bit windy, isn't it?" during a gale is a comical British trope.

The British are masters of many types of humor. In the fourteenth century, Geoffrey Chaucer used irony, parody, and burlesque to great effect in the *Canterbury Tales*. The British delight in verbal dexterity, at every level—from the wit of Oscar Wilde to the elaborate insults of Rowan Atkinson's TV antihero Blackadder. Puns and sexual innuendo appear in both Shakespeare and the nineteenth-century humorous and satirical magazine *Punch*. They are the mainstay of the Ealing Studio's *Carry On* film series and of TV and stand-up comedians such as Julian Clary's risqué routine.

Highlighting socially awkward moments goes down well. Rowan Atkinson's "Mr. Bean" and Ricky Gervais in "The Office" are examples. Situation comedy can be seen in TV series such as "Only Fools and Horses," "Gavin and Stacey," "Peep Show," and "Motherland." Stand-up comedians Jimmy Carr, Peter Kay, and Dawn French excel at observations about the ridiculous or awkward aspects of daily life. There are comedians such as Jack Dee who use dry humor, conveyed without a smile, as a means of making people laugh. Old-fashioned wry or rueful jokes about stereotypically overbearing mothers-in-law are still a comedy staple, even though some people today find them offensive or sexist.

The lampooning of human frailty has a long tradition in this country, going back to the eighteenth-century satires of Alexander Pope and Jonathan Swift, the paintings of William Hogarth, and the caricatures of James Gillray. It is alive and well today in the pointed, unflattering cartoons of politicians in the daily papers. British democracy gives free rein to satirical humor, which the puppet show "Spitting Image" did so well, and the panel shows "Have I Got News for You" and "Mock the Week" still do. In fact, Brits don't shy away from anything taboo—despite the growing fear of offending the politically correct and being "cancelled"—and black humor about dark subjects is a popular genre.

There is humor in cross-dressing, a requirement for all drama in Shakespeare's time. Today it's mostly seen in Christmas pantomime—interactive comical musicals often based on fairy tales such as *Jack and the Beanstalk*, *Cinderella*, and *Puss in Boots*. The "leading boy" (the hero) is played by a pretty young woman and the "wicked stepmother" (the comic character) is played by a middle-aged man in drag—the "pantomime dame."

IDENTITY AND PRIDE IN HERITAGE

With 20,000 scheduled monuments and half a million listed buildings in England, and the UK's thirty-three World Heritage Sites, Britain's extraordinarily rich history is a key component of its national identity. That people take enormous pride in the history that has shaped them is evident in the number of conservation charities: English Heritage, Historic Royal Palaces, Archaeology Scotland, the Welsh Historic Gardens Trust, and Europe's largest conservation charity, the National Trust, which has 5.3 million members—more than the population of Costa Rica.

Despite these expressions of collective civic pride, some Britons underplay, or even undervalue, the sort of public displays of national identity that are highly prized elsewhere in the world.

The Welsh celebrate St. David's Day on March 1 by wearing a national emblem—a daffodil or leek—and organizing concerts at schools, while the Irish mark St. Patrick's day on March 17 around the world. Scots celebrate St. Andrew's Day on November 30 with a national holiday, *cèilidh* (pronounced KAY-lee) folk dances, and traditional dishes such as Cullen skink (fish soup), neeps and tatties (swede and potato), and cranachan (an oatmeal, cream, whisky, and raspberry dessert).

The English, on the other hand, do not observe the feast of St. George—the patron saint of England, famous for slaying a dragon—as a national holiday on April 23. The day used largely to pass unnoticed, but in recent years the United Kingdom Independence Party (UKIP), now Reform UK, has been highlighting its significance.

RELIGION

The indigenous Celts believed in a multiplicity of deities and that rocks, rivers, and trees had spirits. They worshiped in sacred groves or ritual enclosures. They considered bulls, boars, stags, and horses to be sacred, practiced animal sacrifice to appease the gods, bring luck, or ward off evil—occasionally sacrificing slaves and enemies, too—and they believed in life after death.

The Romans introduced Christianity, and it continues to be the dominant religion, with 46 percent of the population in England and Wales, or 27.5 million people, describing themselves as Christian in the 2021 census. The Church of England is the only established Church in Britain, and its members are known as Anglicans. The prime minister advises the monarch on the appointment of its head, the Archbishop of Canterbury.

The Roman Catholic Church continues to have the largest active adult membership of any Christian denomination. Dwindling regular attendance at mass (fewer than one million) has been boosted by immigration. Research by the Christian thinktank Theos in 2020 shows that in London the biggest Christian denomination is Catholic (35 percent of the Christian population), followed by Anglican (33 percent).

Denominational schools, such as Catholic and Church of England schools, are supported by the state in the same way as nondenominational schools. Easter and Christmas, the two most important events in the Christian calendar, are public holidays. At the same time, partly due to a more enlightened view of other faiths by schools and the media, festivals observed by other religions, such as Ramadan (Muslim), Diwali (Hindu), Vaisakhi (Sikh), and Passover (Jewish) are more widely understood and respected.

Churchgoing among Christians has dropped dramatically—to the extent that some observers are now wondering whether Britain as a whole has a majority of believers anymore. The 2021 census revealed that 37 percent of the population in England and Wales (22 million) don't consider themselves religious, an increase of 12 percent since the 2011 census. As church attendance drops, or disappears altogether, many churches have been converted into community centers, apartments, theaters, or even pubs.

There is a significant number of other faiths practiced in Britain, especially Islam, Hinduism, Sikhism, Judaism, and Buddhism, in that order. Religious organizations, including many multifaith groups, are actively involved in volunteer work and the provision of social services.

DUTY AND CHARITY

Generosity, in the form of the desire to donate money or volunteer some time for the benefit of others, is an admirable quality of the British character. There are more than 183,000 charitable organizations registered with the Charity Commission for England and Wales, and six million volunteers. This quality is perhaps best summed up in the person of the late Captain Sir Tom Moore, who, aged ninety-nine, walked a hundred laps of his garden in 2020—a feat which ultimately raised £38 million for NHS charities.

After the government, the greatly respected Salvation Army, founded in London by William Booth in 1865, is the largest provider of social services. Today, this Christian organization works in 134 countries, providing hostels, a family-tracing service, children's and youth programs, as well as services for older people, survivors of trafficking, and alcoholics.

In addition, thousands of other groups come together at community events to support local needs such as social welfare, education, sports, heritage, the environment, and the arts.

Annual national events include Red Nose Day in March—which sees thousands of people buy and wear a red, clown-like nose—which is broadcast on the television channel ITV, while Children in Need in November is backed by a day-long program on the BBC. These events encourage millions of individuals and thousands of companies and community groups to contribute money, time, and skill in entertainment or endurance projects to raise money for charities.

The arrival of the National Lottery in 1994 has had a negative impact on the amount of money given to charities; on the other hand, a significant proportion of the Lottery receipts goes to "good causes."

The World of Amateur Dramatics

The British are perhaps instinctive thespians: they love a good show, including the pomp associated with many public occasions. They love a challenge, they both love "taking part" and are great individualists. No wonder, therefore, that the world of amateur dramatics ("Amdram") continues to be very much alive and well in Britain. Up and down the country you will find local amateur dramatic societies putting on plays, musicals, and other entertainments. According to *The Independent* newspaper, in 2012 some 2,500 amateur dramatic groups around the country put on over 10,000 productions between them.

CLASS

Historically, most British people were born into a rigid social order, a hierarchy of upper-class, middle-class, or working-class families, and most people remained in their societal tier. This class system is depicted in popular period dramas on TV such as "Downton Abbey" and "Bridgerton."

The Upper Class

The upper class generally refers to the aristocracy, the traditional "ruling class"—a privileged, powerful group of people. It largely consists of wealthy families who've benefited from inherited land or property. Many have a peerage—the five titles, ranked in order of importance, being Duke and Duchess, Marquess and Marchioness, Earl and Countess, Viscount and Viscountess, and Baron and Baroness. *Burke's Peerage*, which was established in 1826, is a detailed guide to the pedigrees of titled families, while the monthly magazine *Tatler* has been reporting on the rich and powerful since it was founded in 1709.

The upper class tends to keep itself to itself. Many marriages continue to be "arranged" through carefully managed introductions at weddings, balls, and other social or sporting events that bring together sons and daughters of the "right" background and age.

Those members who find themselves short of cash may open their stately homes to the public and charge an entry fee, or live in impoverished circumstances among priceless antiques.

Members of the upper class are known for their impeccable manners and clear accent, with its sharply defined "ts," distinctive "ohs," and long "a" sounds. King Charles, the Duchess of Cambridge, and the politician Jacob Rees-Mogg have such an accent. This set the standard of educated speech and was prized by the BBC. However, over the past few decades the broadcaster has endeavored to appeal to a range of viewers and listeners by employing presenters with accents from various classes and regions. The British can generally sum up one another's class and where they grew up within moments of meeting.

Studying at private schools such as Eton or Harrow, usually followed by Oxford or Cambridge University, is also an indicator of being upper class, with a first-rate education and access to an influential "old boys' network." Those who work typically become high-ranking officers in the Armed Forces, politicians, or perhaps property developers. Pastimes meanwhile might include traditional country sports such as shooting, fishing, and hunting (though fox hunting was banned in Scotland in 2002 and in England and Wales in 2004 after animal rights campaigned against its cruelty). Many upper-class people also keep horses and ride for pleasure or competitively, including show jumping, and take an interest in racing. They are likely to play or watch polo too.

The Middle Class

The middle classes, whose wealth or occupations put them between the aristocracy and laborers, were and still are typically landowners and "gentlemen," who were later joined by those who made money during or after the Industrial Revolution. Middle-class values formed the backbone of Victorian society and provided the trained professionals who ran the Empire.

These days, the middle class encompasses the managerial and so-called "upwardly mobile" sections of society, as well, perhaps, as a "downwardly mobile" section from the upper class. It is seen to represent the greater part of the population as a whole, certainly in southern England. It is generally less rigid in its behavior and etiquette than the upper class.

Education—at a private, grammar, or respectable state school, preferably followed by university—is important to the middle classes. Middle-class pastimes call for expensive equipment or extensive training, such as skiing, golf, horseback riding, or rugby. It's also common to practice yoga and Pilates at an upmarket gym.

Although they tend to approach life in a more relaxed manner compared to the upper classes, the middle classes also enjoy pomp and pageantry, such as the State Opening of Parliament by the King, garden parties at Buckingham Palace, and royal weddings and jubilees.

The Working Class

The development of the railway, canals, and factories in the eighteenth century created a new industrial working class. While once this term conjured up images of exploitation and social inequality, today it's often used by the main political parties to mean "hard-working people" or even the entire working population. The trade unions that developed at the beginning of the twentieth century to champion workers' rights led to the formation of today's Labour Party.

The working class has its own rituals and etiquette that inform behavior and determine what is expected of its members. Working-class culture is portrayed in TV dramas known as "soaps." The longest running of these, "Coronation Street," and "Hollyoaks" reflect the way of life in the northwest of England, "Emmerdale" depicts daily life in the Yorkshire Dales in the northeast, and "Eastenders" mirrors life in and around London's East End.

When the working classes are not watching TV, they might be found down the local pub, playing snooker or darts in a working men's club (these now accept women), playing soccer (known as football), or "having a flutter" in a betting shop or bingo hall.

In recent decades, the impenetrable hierarchy that once separated the classes has become much more fluid. It's possible for a bright, state-educated working-class child to secure a student loan or scholarship and attend Oxford University, or for a prince to marry a middle-class woman he meets at university, as the present Duke of Cornwall did. Some people distinguish between "old money"—those who have inherited wealth and all the upper-class trappings that come with it—and "new money" or "*nouveaux riches*"—a disparaging term usually used to describe working-class people who have become affluent by establishing a successful business or through a lottery win or crime, but who do not have the accent, education, or social polish of their associates.

People often feel more comfortable associating with others from the same background. A working-class person might feel uncomfortable at a "society" wedding, for example, as might an aristocrat in a betting shop. But a certain amount of self-confidence would carry the day for both. There may also be consequences for mixing above or below your "grade." A member of the working class, for example, might be teased for joining an expensive health club, which is seen as middle class, as might a noble who develops a taste for bingo.

The "Honours" List

Britain has a public awards system known as "honours," which confers recognition on worthy individuals, regardless of their class or wealth. Anyone, from a diplomat, politician, or civil servant to a sports star, artist, entrepreneur, or community champion, may be publicly recognized in this way for their outstanding contribution to society.

The Honours Lists, as they are called, are announced twice a year. The New Year's Honours are published in late December and the King's Birthday Honours are published on the King's official birthday in June.

The New Year list is largely compiled by the prime minister of the day, advised by ministers and civil servants. The King's Birthday list is also assembled by ministers and civil servants, along with input from the King and his advisors.

There are many levels of honours, from peerages down to minor awards. While this means that people from all walks of life can aspire to elevation, titles are so broadly conferred today that some people feel their inherent value has depreciated. Some members of the Labour Party would like to see the entire honours system abolished.

HIGH CULTURE OR LOW CULTURE?

"High" culture is typically associated with the upper classes and "low" culture with the masses. Expensive and sophisticated, high culture often requires a certain level of knowledge, training, or critical thinking to interpret and appreciate it, which may be considered challenging, dry, or pretentious to people without such skills. The elite meanwhile may look down upon certain forms of low culture, such as pop music or reality TV, which attract others for their accessibility or convenience. Culture can, therefore, be divisive.

While fashion is a matter of taste and comfort, *haute couture*, or custom-made designer clothing, also demonstrates craftsmanship and the wealth of the wearer. The opposite—fast fashion—is affordable, mass-produced clothing designed to last less than a year.

Like *haute couture*, ballet, art, opera, classical music, and performances of Shakespeare's plays are widely perceived as being only for the rich. However, low-priced tickets to the BBC Proms or Shakespeare's Globe are often available, and entrance to most public museums and galleries, including the British Museum in London, remains free.

The arts in Britain continue to flourish, partly because of the strength of native talent and creativity, and partly because of the support they receive from national fundraising associations such as the Art Fund and Arts Council England, which invests public money from the government and the National Lottery in cultural institutions. The great British temples to the arts, such as the National Gallery and the Royal Opera House in London, or the Royal Scottish Academy in Edinburgh, are outstanding examples of their kind.

SOME VIRTUES, VICES, AND QUIRKS

The British love nature, language, and wit—and apologizing. If you stand on someone's toe by mistake, don't be surprised if *they're* the first to say "sorry."

The common expression "there's a time and a place for everything" suggests a need for harmony and order. The latter is reinforced daily by the general manager of the House of Commons, the Speaker, who calls or shouts "Order! Order!" (always twice) to silence over-excited Members of Parliament during debates.

The British like to fit in with those around them and one reflection of this is the wearing of their traditional national costume. While the Scots have tartan and kilts and the Welsh tall black hats, dresses called "bedgowns," and red woollen shawls, England has no national dress. Yet the English love uniforms. Most school children wear uniforms; Morris dancers dress in white shirts and trousers decorated with ribbons at English country fairs; the military don regalia for grand state occasions, while the Yeomen Warders (or Beefeaters) guarding the Tower of London still wear distinctive red and black tunics.

As well as strengthening a sense of social cohesion, uniforms are a manifestation of loyalty—another British trait that's epitomized in the intensely tribal support of local football clubs.

Despite which, Britons cherish their individuality— hence the expression "my home is my castle." They celebrate the arcane, the idiosyncratic, and the eccentric, as shown by their quirky regional festivals and in newspaper stories about madcap inventors.

Creative, practical, and curious by nature, the British are resilient and self-sufficient. These qualities, along with the emphasis placed on individual fulfillment during the Thatcher and Blair years, have prompted a huge expansion of entrepreneurial activity.

Despite their virtues, Britons can sometimes appear to have an air of "superiority." Their self-control and unwillingness to show emotion in the face of difficulties—having a "stiff upper lip"—can also make them seem repressed or reserved. A 2012 YouGov poll, however, found many disputing this characterization— pointing to the public outpouring of grief after the death of Diana, Princess of Wales, and the ready display of emotions on reality TV, or after one too many pints.

This brings us to another vice: Brits can be too fond of alcohol. As a by-product of the "pub culture" it is not uncommon to see men and women stumbling home, vomiting or urinating in public after drinking to excess on a night out (see page 109). This may appear to be something of a paradox, given the natural reserve of so many British people; one possible explanation is that they drink to shed their inhibitions.

The British are skeptical and anti-intellectual, and may be dismissive, mistrustful, or openly hostile toward experts, as seen in the national Covid-19 vaccine debate that raged in 2021 and beyond. The 2021 census also revealed that only 35 percent of the UK population trust national government, lower than the 41 percent average across the thirty-eight member countries of the Organization for Economic Co-operation and Development. Perhaps this skepticism is reinforced by a certain stubbornness, or, as a Brit might say, "bloody-mindedness."

ATTITUDES TOWARD SEX

Historically, attitudes toward sex have never been straightforward. This ambivalence has sometimes generated extreme outcomes—from periods of repression, as in the Puritan Commonwealth of Oliver Cromwell (1653–58), or the reign of Queen Victoria (1837–1901), when some people even covered piano legs out of a perverse notion of modesty, to periods of excess, as in the Regency period of the early nineteenth century, or, some might say, today.

Sex and sexual repression have been a major preoccupation of British writers, dramatists, artists, entertainers, and social reformers for generations—the long-running farce in London's West End, *No Sex, Please, We're British* (1971–87) is a classic example of its genre. During the 1960s Britain experienced a so-called "sexual liberation," which resulted in higher divorce rates, greater sexual freedom, more sexually transmitted infections, and diseases such as AIDS in the 1980s.

Some visitors may be shocked at Britain's open attitude to sex today. Written and broadcast media support sexual freedom in terms of choice and orientation, and explicit sex scenes in TV dramas are now common, as are sex-related humor and articles in magazines or broadsheet newspapers and websites.

Most Britons still prefer to keep their sex lives private, although others record themselves and post the videos on the subscription site OnlyFans, which attracted more than a billion monthly visitors worldwide in 2022.

Queer Britain

The term "queer," originally derogatory, has been defiantly embraced by the gay community since the 1980s. Today it simply means not identifying as a heterosexual male or female. Homosexual behavior has been documented in virtually every civilization, in the case of Britain dating back to Celtic times. The monarchs Edward II (1307–27), James I (1603–25), and Queen Anne (1702–14) are believed to have been gay and lesbian. The author E. M. Forster, playwright Noël Coward, and mathematician and codebreaker

Alan Turing—whom the government infamously chemically castrated in 1952, only to pardon him posthumously—were all gay too. Turing is now a hero, and his image is printed on £50 banknotes.

In 1533 male homosexuality became illegal, and was punishable by death until 1861. Being labeled a homosexual could result in a prison sentence, and the stigma was enough to destroy careers, relationships, and reputations. In 1895 the flamboyant playwright Oscar Wilde famously sued his gay lover's father for libel, which ultimately resulted in Wilde being convicted of gross indecency and sentenced to two years' hard labor.

While laws against homosexuality began to change in the liberal 1960s, attitudes lagged behind—illustrated by the hostile press and public reaction to pop singer George Michael being caught in a sting by an undercover police officer in the US in 1998. Attitudes have changed since then, with the introduction of the 2004 Civil Partnership Act allowing same-sex couples to enter legal partnerships, and the 2013 Marriage (Same-Sex Couples) Act allowing non-heterosexual marriages in England and Wales. Scotland followed in 2014, and Northern Ireland in 2019.

Today, it is broadly accepted that many people identify as non-binary, or as someone who feels they have no, multiple, or fluctuating genders. They may be lesbian, gay, bisexual, transgender, queer/questioning, intersex, asexual (LGBTIQA+), or something else.

Public acceptance of the gay community began with the first UK Pride festival, which took place in London in 1972. Since then, people and national businesses have shown support by flying rainbow flags. The National Centre for Social Research corroborates this change in attitudes, revealing that 67 percent of British people believe that sexual relations between adults of the same sex are not wrong, compared to 17 percent in 1983. London and Brighton have particularly strong queer communities.

In 2021, for the first time, the census in England and Wales asked respondents over the age of sixteen voluntary questions about sexual orientation and gender identity. It found that 89 percent (43 million) identified as straight or heterosexual; 3 percent (1.5 million) as gay, lesbian, bisexual, or another sexual orientation; and 0.5 percent (262,000 people) identified with a gender that was different from what was registered on their birth certificate (6 percent didn't answer). Of the 0.5 percent, 48,000 identified as a trans man, 48,000 as a trans woman, and 30,000 as non-binary. About 18,000 chose an alternative identity, and 118,000 didn't provide an identity. The Queer Britain museum, which opened in London's King's Cross in 2022, explores this topic further.

CHAPTER FOUR

CUSTOMS & TRADITIONS

POMP AND PAGEANTRY

Britain's historical ceremonies are a grand form of public theater, attracting people from across the country and visitors from abroad. During the State Opening of Parliament, for example, the king travels to the Palace of Westminster in a magnificent horse-drawn state coach, and, dressed in royal robes, delivers a speech from the throne of the House of Lords. Lords, ladies, judges, and officers of the House, wear red robes, gowns, or uniforms; the military their regimental uniforms with medals on display, and the members of the House of Commons in formal "morning suits." The Trooping the Colour is also a spectacular sight, with thousands of parading soldiers, horses, and musicians. As Commander-in-Chief of the Armed Forces, the king receives his new regiment of guards to mark his official birthday on the second Saturday in June.

Domestic traditions such as exchanging presents on Christmas Day are passed down through the generations and observed by the majority of Britons, while specific customs are widely accepted ways of doing something in a particular place or time, such as Maypole dancing in May. A key part of being British is to follow traditions and customs—or, at the very least, respect them.

NATIONAL FESTIVALS AND EVENTS

Many national festivals are marked with a public holiday. New Year's Day marks the beginning of the new calendar year, on January 1. Most people go for a walk or relax at home, while London celebrates with a New Year's Day Parade.

Some Christians observe parts or all of Holy Week, which takes place the week before Easter in March or April. Palm Sunday marks the beginning of the week. It commemorates the crowds waving palm branches as Jesus Christ entered Jerusalem. The next day, Holy Monday, Jesus cursed a fig tree for not bearing fruit, which, it is believed, symbolized the people who had abandoned the true path. Jesus predicted his death on Holy Tuesday, while Holy Wednesday marks the day Judas betrayed him. Maundy Thursday commemorates the Last Supper, Jesus' final meal. Good Friday is the day the Romans crucified him. Some Christians mark the day by going to church or attending a passion play, which reenacts Jesus' last moments; at tea time they eat spiced "hot cross buns." Christians celebrate the Resurrection on Easter Sunday by attending a church service. Families paint eggs (a symbol of new life), children hunt for hidden Easter eggs, and there is Simnel cake for tea.

The Ancient Celts celebrated the beginning of summer on May 1 with bonfires, dances, and feasts. Since 1978, the first Monday in May has been a national holiday. On May Day villages and market towns host dances and parades led by a May Queen—a girl dressed in white and crowned with flowers.

Bonfire Night falls on November 5. This dates back to the events of 1605, when Catholic dissidents planned to assassinate the members of Parliament and the Protestant king, James I, by blowing up the House

The Green Man and the May Queen at the local Green Man Festival in Clun, Shropshire.

of Lords. A ringleader of the infamous "Gunpowder Plot," Guy Fawkes, was caught red-handed and hanged, drawn, and quartered. To celebrate the foiling of the plot, people have made effigies ("guys"), lit bonfires, and set off fireworks ever since.

Remembrance Sunday, the second Sunday in November, commemorates the sacrifice of British and Commonwealth servicemen and women in the two World Wars and later conflicts. It is marked with parades, silences, and wreath-laying ceremonies at war memorials throughout the country. Artificial red poppies are worn in remembrance of the fields of Flanders, where tens of thousands died in the First World War.

Most Britons celebrate Christmas on December 25 whether they're religious or not. In the weeks leading up to it people buy presents for loved ones, hold Christmas parties with friends and coworkers, decorate Christmas

Up Helly Aa. After the burning of the longship, parties go on into the night.

trees with lights, and open windows in Advent calendars. On Christmas Day they exchange presents, play festive music and games, and enjoy a traditional Christmas dinner.

Scots call New Year's Eve Hogmanay. As well as fireworks, dancing, and the singing of "Auld Lang Syne," there is a torchlit procession in Edinburgh in which participants wear helmets and carry shields in a nod to Britain's Viking past. In the Shetlands, the end of the Yule season is marked by Up Helly Aa, a winter fire festival that culminates in 1,000 people carrying flaming torches through Lerwick and burning a replica Norse longship.

PUBLIC HOLIDAYS

On public or "bank" holidays banks and shops are usually closed or have reduced opening times, there is no postal service, and public transportation runs a limited service. The holidays are:

January 1 New Year's Day

March/April Good Friday

March/April Easter Monday

First Monday in May May Day

Last Monday in May Spring bank holiday

Last Friday in August Summer bank holiday

November 30 St. Andrew's Day (Scotland only)

December 25 Christmas Day

December 26 Boxing Day

FOLK CULTURE

Britain's rural communities have a wealth of folklore and local cultural practices and activities. These take many forms—from traditional Orkney chair-making in the Scottish Isles to the Cornish belief in mischievous piskeys (pixies) being lucky. Battle reenactments, storytelling, and harvest festivals in the fall take place around the country.

To herald the arrival of spring, people traditionally danced around a Maypole hung with colorful ribbons, which, by the end of the dance, would form a pattern. Maypole dances still take place in some market towns.

Morris dancing, which dates back to the mid-1400s, is another feature of spring festivals. The dance creates choreographed patterns, executed by men wearing white with bells on their shins, and involves rhythmic stepping, waving handkerchiefs, clapping sticks, and yelping. Today these dances take place outdoors at country fairs and village fêtes.

Summer fêtes typically take place on a village green decorated with bunting. There are stalls selling homemade cakes such as Victoria sponge, which might be made for a competition. Traditional entertainments include Punch and Judy puppet shows, coconut shies, tug of war contests, and tombolas—participants purchase a raffle ticket, and if their number is picked out of the revolving drum, they win a prize.

Britain's folk festivals have taken place since medieval times. The annual Cooper's Hill Cheese Roll in Gloucestershire is about six hundred years old: a wheel of Double Gloucester cheese is rolled at 70 mph (113 kmph) down the hill as participants chase after it—the first to reach the bottom wins the cheese.

"Jack in the Green" began in the 1600s as a contest between milkmaids and chimney sweeps. The name describes the man who, covered in foliage and topped with a floral crown, leads a procession through the streets of the East Sussex town of Hastings every May, accompanied by live bands, drummers, and dancers.

The World Bog Snorkelling Championships in Wales are another British quirk. Participants in snorkels and flippers race through water-filled peat bogs every August.

Scottish and Irish *cèilidhean* (cèilidhs) and English country or barn dances are communal affairs. Often, a caller provides instructions before the dance and band begin, and men, women, and children of all ages weave intricate patterns, sometimes in circles or down a line in pairs. The Scottish "Gay Gordons" is a particularly well-known example.

Like dances, folk crafts are another example of Britain's intangible cultural heritage. Aging artisans, limited apprenticeships, and mass production have threatened the British folk craft tradition, but it receives support from Heritage Crafts, which highlights those at risk of dying out, such as Fair Isle straw-backed chairs and Sussex trugs (willow garden baskets). Corn dollies, Cornish hedging, and Shetland lace knitting are all endangered, while dry stone walling, Harris tweed weaving, and making Highland pipes are in a healthy state, with enough craftspeople to pass on their skills. There are craft centers throughout the country, such as Derbyshire's Museum of Making, where craftsmen and women demonstrate their skills and sell their products, from wood turning to pottery and pewter work.

TEA

Although tea is now a great British institution, it was introduced by Dutch traders in the 1650s, when it first became fashionable among royalty and the nobility. In 1664 the East India Company began to import tea for the upper classes, and when tea taxes were slashed in 1783 consumption rocketed among the masses.

The term "tea" can be confusing. It may mean just a cup of tea, drunk with or without milk, sugar, or lemon, or served strong—"builder's tea"—often with a biscuit. Increasingly, it may also refer to floral or fruity infusions.

"Tea" can also mean a light meal at about 4:00 p.m. Anna, the seventh Duchess of Bedford, introduced this in 1840 after feeling peckish between lunch and dinner. Her custom of snacking on bread and butter, cake, and tea in her drawing room with her friends spread to the Victorian and Edwardian upper classes. Today many hotels serve tea and champagne alongside crustless sandwiches, warm scones with jam and clotted cream, and bitesize pastries on a tiered, fine china stand on a low table.

"High tea" or, in northern England, simply "tea," means an early cooked meal for the family after school and work, served at a high table at about 6:00 p.m.

English tea with a selection of cakes and sandwiches.

A "cream tea" is a delicious variant of afternoon tea. It consists of scones with jam and clotted cream, a specialty of the West Country (Devon and Cornwall).

PUB CULTURE

Pubs, or public houses, were and to a great extent still are the backbone of Britain's social life. Britain's oldest pub, Ye Olde Fighting Cocks in Hertfordshire, dates back to 793, while The Tabard in London was mentioned in Chaucer's *Canterbury Tales* six hundred years ago. The Industrial Revolution was "lubricated" with alcohol; the great national projects, like the building of the railways and the docks of London and Liverpool, could not have been completed without it. Today, social drinking continues to be part of the British way of life. Unfortunately, excessive drinking among young adults has been a developing problem for the police and health authorities (see pages 95–6).

The Churchill Arms pub in London.

Pub names such as The Queen's Arms or The Ship Inn often reflect their history. Typically, the name is painted on a sign swinging by the front door. A traditional country pub might feature a flagstone floor, beamed ceiling, thatched roof, wooden bar, and a fireplace. Many also have beer gardens—picnic benches on a lawn or in a courtyard. Snooker and darts are common, as are televisions screening live sports and, since the mid-1980s, coin-operated game machines. Pub quizzes with prizes are also popular.

Beer, ale, and cider have always been in demand, and the Campaign for Real Ale (CAMRA) has been championing small, independent breweries since 1971.

Gin was introduced to Britain in the Middle Ages. A gin craze in the 1700s meant that social issues soared until the 1751 Gin Act curbed consumption of the spirit, which was dubbed "Mother's ruin." Relaxed EU regulations in 2008 led to a boom in craft distilleries and the current "Ginaissance." Gin-based Pimm's was first served in 1840. Pimm's No. 1 Cup, mixed with lemonade, strawberries, cucumber, mint, and other fruit, is commonly drunk in summer.

Like Champagne, Prosecco, and Cava, the origin of English and Welsh Quality Sparkling Wine is protected, and it is growing in popularity. In 2023 there were 943 vineyards and 209 wineries in Britain, some of which are owned by French Champagne houses such as Taittinger. Wine bars offer a greater variety of Old World and New World wines than pubs.

It's good pub etiquette to take turns to pay for your companions' drinks, known as "buying rounds." This, along with drinking games and a legal drinking age of eighteen, has given rise to the British reputation for drinking to excess. Strict drunk driving laws, however, make driving when drunk a taboo.

Despite all of this, pubs are in decline. In 2007 smoking was banned in all enclosed public places. This, along with staff from the EU leaving the country after Brexit, the impact of Covid-19, soaring energy bills, and a growing wellness trend, means that in 2021 there were 45,800 pubs in the UK, compared to 60,800 in 2000.

While traditional pubs serve affordable dishes such as pies, scampi and chips, and a ploughman's lunch—a board loaded with cheese, bread, pickled onions, celery, and a boiled egg—since the 1990s many have reinvented themselves as "gastropubs" with restaurant-quality cuisine.

CHAPTER FIVE

MAKING FRIENDS

FRIENDSHIP

The long-held view of the British as being cold, or even rude, to foreigners, particularly in the cities, is unfounded. It is not always challenging for non-British people to make friends with locals, and friendships once formed can be valued and permanent.

As elsewhere, friendships in Britain are usually formed by repeated exposure to the same people, in the local pub or place of worship, for example. Friends of friends are likely to be less guarded than strangers.

A word of caution, though. Today it is common practice to use first names in many areas of everyday life, even with your boss or a client. This is based on the assumption that informality makes everyone feel more comfortable and relaxed—but this doesn't necessarily equate with friendship or a desire to spend more time together outside work.

POLITENESS

The new informality does not always apply, and the terms "Sir" and "Madam" are still used in some shops, the Armed Services, and luxury hotels.

In daily life, British people show respect by being on time, standing in line (or "queueing"), and regularly saying "please," "thank you," "excuse me," and "sorry"—even when they're not at fault.

It's also important to master the art of small talk, to break the ice or build rapport, although the opposite is true on the London Underground. Ultimately, being polite is consideration of other peoples' feelings at all times. This can range from not playing music aloud in public to opening a door for a stranger or attending a social event with coworkers even if you don't feel like it.

Etiquette evolves with the times, so today it's advisable to avoid checking or answering your phone in the company of others. Social media can magnify rudeness. It has, of course, always been rude to "ghost" someone—end communication between friends or fail to keep a date without giving a reason. Today the ability to meet people online who don't know the rest of your social circle has made ghosting easier and more prevalent.

GREETINGS AND TOPICS OF CONVERSATION

Common informal greetings are "Hi," "Hey," or "Y'alright?". "Hello" is acceptable in all situations, while good morning, good afternoon, or good evening are more formal. "How are you?" is also customary among family, coworkers, friends, or acquaintances, to which the typical response would be, "Fine, thank you, how are you?"—even if the speaker is anything but fine. "How do you do?" is a much more formal greeting used when being introduced. The response is the same, "How do you do."

A firm handshake with the right hand is routine in a business setting or among acquaintances or strangers. A limp handshake is considered insincere or sloppy.

On social occasions, say at a dinner party with colleagues and their partners, men and women kiss on the cheek or make a "mmuh" kissing sound in the air near the cheek. One kiss is most common, but some people kiss both cheeks, which leads to some awkwardness. Hugging is fairly typical these days as a way of saying hello or good-bye, particularly among younger people.

When it comes to what to talk about, the weather is a safe bet. Depending on the situation, Britons may also ask someone how their journey was, or whether they'd like a cup of tea or water. When meeting people for the first time, it's advisable to avoid contentious subjects such as politics, religion, money, or sex, and not to ask questions about their age, weight, relationship status, or whether or not they want children. These subjects can trigger upset, and it's also considered inappropriate to show emotion in public. To end a conservation with someone you've just met, it's polite to say, "Nice to meet you."

TERMS OF ENDEARMENT

Visitors to Britain are sometimes surprised to be addressed in rather intimate terms. In southern England, on the buses and in the shops, you may well be addressed as "love," "lovey," "dear," "darling," "pet," or "petal"—and perhaps, if you are lucky, "my lover" in Devon.

As you go north you will hear different terms, such as "chuck" (around Liverpool and the northwest), "duck" (around Sheffield and the northwest), and "hen" (in Scotland).

As a market trader weighs some apples for you, he or she might say, "Just over a kilo. All right, darlin'?" These are old-fashioned terms of endearment that aren't intended to offend, although some modern women find them patronizing and insulting.

MEETING NEW PEOPLE

The best way to find people you have something in common with is through an activity where you will see them on a regular basis, such as a weekly cooking or language class. You may form stronger bonds more quickly if the activity involves a commitment, such as a team sport, choir, amateur theater, or volunteering, as the others in the group will expect you to show up, rely on you to attend, and miss you if you don't.

Common sense applies. You're more likely to connect with acquaintances on a deeper level if you smile, take an interest in them, ask and answer questions so that you listen and talk in equal amounts, and do people favors. You may have to persevere somewhat, and if your efforts are persistently not reciprocated, give up!

Most people don't talk to one another at the gym, unless they recognize each other from group classes such as circuits.

INVITATIONS HOME

If invited to someone's home for dinner aim to arrive on time or no more than five to ten minutes late. Do not arrive early in case your host isn't ready for you. Arrive too late, and the meal may be served cold.

Wear comfortable, smart casual attire. If your host is not wearing shoes, take your shoes off. If they are wearing shoes, it's polite to ask if you should take yours off. Your host may offer you slippers.

It is usual to bring a gift, such as flowers, chocolates, or wine if you know your host drinks alcohol. These do not have to be expensive, but they should be attractive and good quality. Your host may not open the wine in front of you but will appreciate it all the same. Visitors coming to stay for a few nights or from overseas would do well to bring a gift for the parents and, perhaps, appropriate little presents typical of their hometown or region for the children.

It's good manners to ask your hosts if they need any help preparing setting the table. It's also polite to wait to be seated or to be served or offered a second helping.

Your host will appreciate an offer to help clear the table, or load the dishwasher at the end, although they will usually decline it.

Always thank your hosts shortly after such an occasion, via text, social media, a phone call, or by sending a short note, which is the formal way. It would also be polite to offer to return the favor one day.

Polite Conversation

As already mentioned, if you are unsure of your company avoid saying anything that might cause offense or embarrassment. The traditional taboo subjects used to be politics, sex, and religion, as they can cause ill-feeling or raise tempers, and so disturb the atmosphere around the dinner table or down the pub. Today there is more leeway. Money is also off limits among acquaintances or colleagues, most of whom would never discuss their salaries. Even close friends, family members, and some life partners don't discuss their salaries, investments, or savings with one another.

Displays of wealth are unlikely to impress and are generally regarded as showing off. On the other hand, it is perfectly acceptable to talk about how you have managed to save in small ways—such as finding a bottle of good wine at half price in a supermarket.

TABLE MANNERS

When eating, it's good manners to hold the knife in your right hand and the fork in your left, with the prongs facing down. Rest them on the plate between mouthfuls, while talking, and straight together in a 6:30 p.m. position to indicate you've finished eating. Some people have adopted the habit of cutting up their food first and then eating it with just the fork, which traditionalists will frown upon. Use a fork, and possibly a spoon, for eating spaghetti. Don't burp or slurp, chew with your mouth open, talk with your mouth full, or waste too much food, particularly if you're a guest.

DATING

While it used to be the norm in heterosexual relationships for the man to court the woman, organize dates, and pick up the bill, these days it depends on the couple. It's perfectly acceptable for a woman to make the first move—and the dating app Bumble enforces this. Traditional heterosexual couples may still prefer the man to choose a venue for a first date, although most couples decide together. To remain safe, it's sensible to use public transportation to get to and from the date, go on early dates in public places, and keep an eye on your drink to prevent it being spiked with drugs. Some bars and clubs, particularly in London and Lincolnshire, encourage women to "Ask for Angela" if they're feeling uncomfortable on a date, and staff will assist them.

CHAPTER SIX

AT HOME

HOUSING

Britain's housing stock today reflects a wide variety of architectural styles. Tudor houses built between the mid-1400s and mid-1500s feature thatched roofs and exposed timber frames; today these are most common in villages or preserved as visitor attractions.

In the 1600s, the Dutch Golden Age influenced Stuart architecture, which led to the rise of gabled dormers (windows in a roof). There was also a move toward stone and brick and more two-story homes.

The neoclassical Georgian homes of the 1700s meanwhile were influenced by ancient Greece, so they are symmetrical, with cream or white façades often featuring columns.

Between the 1830s and 1900, the Victorians favored asymmetric architecture built in the Gothic Revival style, with pointed arches, and ornate, red brick

Stucco-fronted Victorian terrace house in Notting Hill, London.

exteriors, while the working classes lived in back-to-back terraced housing or purpose-built tenements.

By the 1920s, new archaeological discoveries in Egypt led to a craze for Egyptian motifs such as fans and geometric patterns, which, along with flat roofs and curved windows, came to characterize the Art Deco era.

The postwar building boom of the 1930s saw an explosion of three-bedroom semi-detached houses with pebbledash exteriors and curved bay windows in the suburbs.

After the Second World War the government built blocks of affordable rented apartments (or flats) known as council houses. This peaked in the 1950s, particularly in the new towns on the outskirts of London. More social housing was built in the '60s and '70s in the form of tower blocks and open-plan terraces. Chimneys became obsolete as central heating became common.

By the 1990s, new builds with traditional features such as mock timber frames became popular, a style which has been rejected in the twenty-first century.

Today, open-plan houses or apartments feature steel, glass walls or large windows, and solar panels. Rooms are much smaller than they once were, and ceilings much lower.

The belief that "An Englishman's home is his castle" led to a move toward more people owning their home instead of renting in the 1960s. The prime minister Margaret Thatcher encouraged this by introducing the Housing Act 1980, which gave council house tenants the right to buy their home at a discount. However, while most Britons still aspire to have a mortgage and own their home outright, a housing shortage and soaring house prices are making this dream increasingly unlikely.

The Museum of the Home (formerly the Geoffrye Museum) in Hoxton, East London, explores home life across Britain from 1600 to the present day.

THE FAMILY

Marriage

In a huge societal shift, divorce rates in Britain are rocketing, marriage rates are plummeting, and those who choose to marry are waiting longer to tie the knot.

The number of heterosexual men and women getting married in England and Wales roughly halved between 1991 and 2019—the same year opposite-sex couples were allowed to form a civil partnership. Scotland has also seen a steady decline in the number of people getting married since a peak in 1940.

The Civil Partnership Act 2004 legally recognized same-sex relationships, while the Marriage (Same Sex Couples) Act 2013 allowed same-sex marriage. Civil partnerships in the UK have fluctuated since 2005, but were at their highest in twelve years in 2020. The average age to get married is thirty-five for heterosexual men, thirty-three for heterosexual women, thirty-eight for gay men, and thirty-five for lesbians.

The proportion of adults who have never married or been in a civil partnership has increased every decade in England and Wales, from 26 percent in 1991 to 38 percent in 2021. Divorce rates increased during the same period, from 6 to 9 percent. More people are living alone as well. Religious ceremonies are in decline, favored by 15 percent of all couples, while civil ceremonies are increasing.

Children

Women in England and Wales had, on average, 1.61 children in 2021, the first time the fertility rate has increased since 2012. But more women are having children later, partly because of the cost-of-living crisis. With both parents likely to be working full or part time, and grandparents not living as close to their children as they once did, parents require childcare—and the average annual cost of a full-time nursery place for a child under two in Britain soared to £14,836 in 2023.

Some parents give their older children pocket money so they can learn the value of money and save up for something they want—typically clothes and trainers, technology, confectionery, or makeup.

Many children have their own smartphone, tablet, or gaming device, and access to the internet and social media has transformed their lives. As well as using the internet to do research for homework, many teenagers spend hours each day playing games, watching videos, messaging friends, or watching pornography. Unregulated access to the internet has led to a wave of problems, from an increase in shortsightedness, online bullying, negative personal perceptions, and unwanted sexual messages, to children chatting to strangers online and meeting them offline.

However, the advent of the internet and social media, together with developments in the traditional media and more enlightened educationalists, also means that British children today are better informed and more engaged than their parents were at the same age. They are encouraged to think about topical issues, have opinions, and speak their minds, and tend to be much more articulate than previous generations. Young people such as the Swedish teenager Greta Thunberg, who went viral in 2018 when she skipped school to strike against climate change, and Soma Sara, who founded the anti-rape movement Everyone's Invited in 2020, have been major influences.

At sixteen, children can legally go to the pub on their own and be served non-alcoholic drinks, have sex, and marry, with parental permission. At seventeen they can hold a driver's license, and at eighteen they can vote, purchase alcohol, vapes, and tobacco, and join the Armed Services.

Today families rarely sit and eat meals together, a result of both parents working and children participating in after-school activities. The evening meal will often be something quick and easy—such as a ready-made microwave meal or a takeout, perhaps eaten while sitting on the sofa and watching a program on TV or an electronic device.

PETS

For many British people pets are part of the family. A dog may be treated to a day spa, and cats may sleep in their owner's bed. Newspapers report on families risking their lives to save their pets from drowning or house fires. According to the vet charity PDSA, 53 percent of adults in the UK owned a pet in 2023. Of these, 29 percent had a dog—that's eleven million pet pooches. Around 24 percent had a cat, with four in ten cat owners having more than one. About 2 percent of the population had a rabbit (1.1 million rabbits).

Unfortunately, many people underestimate the amount of time, money, and energy needed to look after pets, particularly dogs. Every year charities such as the Royal Society for the Prevention of Cruelty to Animals advise people to avoid buying pets as a present with the festive message, "A dog is not just for Christmas; it is for life." Still, thousands of unwanted dogs end up on the streets and in temporary care homes such as the Battersea Dogs' Home in London.

The "animal rights" movement has had a considerable impact on government policy; for example, research on live animals is now banned in the cosmetics industry but is allowed under strict rules for scientific research for the benefit of human welfare.

The Pet Travel Scheme, launched by the British government in 2000, allows microchipped pet cats, dogs, and ferrets with a pet passport—or a health certificate to show it has been vaccinated against rabies—to enter or return to Britain from most European countries.

Dogs may also require a tapeworm treatment depending on the country they're visiting. There are no restrictions on bringing in pet rodents, rabbits, invertebrates, amphibians, or reptiles to Britain from EU countries, although birds need a health certificate. There are different rules and quarantine requirements for pets coming to Britain from outside the EU.

EDUCATION

Babies and young children whose parents or guardians are employed may attend one of Britain's 14,000 day-nurseries, nursery schools, preschools, or children's centers. Most are not free.

Home schooling is permitted but rare. Guardians are not required to follow the national curriculum, which is an agreed set of subjects and standards. Most children attend state schools, which are funded by the government and inspected and regulated by Ofsted in England, Estyn in Wales, and Education Scotland in Scotland. Academies, independent schools run by a trust, also receive state funding and are free but don't have to follow the national curriculum.

Primary school students on a class trip.

Children aged five to sixteen are entitled to free education in state schools. Elementary (primary) school is from five to eleven, while high (secondary) school is from eleven to sixteen. English, Welsh, and Scottish schools each follow their own national curriculum. At sixteen, students take General Certificate of Secondary Education (GCSEs) exams in England and Wales, or a Scottish Qualifications Certificate in Scotland. The British education system encourages students to question and debate, rather than learn by rote.

Between sixteen and eighteen, young people are encouraged to stay in full-time education at a sixth form or college, become an apprentice, or combine volunteering, training, and studying. Most students sit A-Level exams at eighteen in England and Wales or Scottish Highers in Scotland.

University undergraduate courses take around three years and are not free. Tuition fees for the 2023–24 academic year were around £9,000, although Scottish

Graduating sudents at the University of Cambridge.

students can study free in Scotland. UK residents who are full-time undergraduates are eligible for a student loan, which they have to pay back after they start work. Postgraduate students can apply for a postgraduate master's loan or postgraduate doctoral loan. The British education system is respected worldwide, as shown by the number of foreign students opting to study here.

HEALTH CARE

The National Health Service, created after the Second World War, is so highly regarded that it is politically untouchable. Registering with a NHS doctor (a GP, or general practitioner) is free. NHS prescriptions are free in many circumstances, including for under-sixteens, sixteen- to eighteen-year-olds in full-time education, the over sixties, expectant mothers, people on income support, or with conditions such as diabetes or epilepsy.

People with life-threatening injuries or symptoms will be taken by ambulance to a local hospital's accident and emergency (A&E) department. Government targets require ambulances to respond to the most serious calls within seven minutes, although there is concern that these targets have been missed, particularly since the 2021 pandemic.

Treatment by an NHS dentist is free in some circumstances, for example, for children under eighteen, people under nineteen in full-time education, pregnant women or new mothers, or people on low-income benefits. However, accessing an NHS dentist in a timely manner is a growing issue. A 2023 YouGov survey of 2,104 people across the UK found that a fifth of Britons are not registered with an NHS dentist, mostly because they can't find one that accepts new patients. As a result, one in ten Britons have attempted to do dental work on themselves.

Long waiting lists have also encouraged Britons to become medical tourists, with the Office for National Statistics estimating that about 248,000 UK residents went abroad for medical treatment in 2019—more than double the figures for 2015.

SMOKING

Since 2007, smoking has been banned in all public indoor spaces. Office workers desperate for a cigarette can be seen puffing away outside on the sidewalk. Pub landlords raised concerns that the ban would have a negative impact on business, but most got around the problem by improving their outdoor spaces or developing their food sales. The drop in the number of adult smokers (over eighteen) has been dramatic; in 2021, 13.3 percent of the adult population, or 6.6 million people, smoked cigarettes. This is the lowest number since records began in 2011. Men, particularly young men without qualifications, are more likely to be smokers. Around 7.7 percent of Britons aged sixteen and over, or 4 million people, also smoke e-cigarettes, despite the government's vigorous anti-smoking campaigns.

WORK AND LEISURE

Most British people in full-time employment work 36 hours a week; however, checking emails or answering work calls out of hours is becoming more common. Generally people take up to an hour's lunch break. Once eating a home-prepared packed lunch at work was the norm. Today more working people are buying their lunches from supermarkets, restaurants, or food stalls.

After work the average Briton might work out in a gym once or twice a week and spend the rest of their spare time scrolling the internet on their smartphones or watching television. However, since 2020 there has been a decline in the watching of terrestrial TV as more people are turning to on-demand streaming services such as Amazon Prime Video, Apple TV, Disney+, and Netflix. These services have also impacted on how often people go to the cinema.

People enjoying an after-work drink near Borough Market, London.

Mid-week treats might include a few drinks in a pub with friends or dinner in a local restaurant. Italian cuisine tops the popularity charts, followed by Chinese, British, Indian, and Mexican food.

At weekends, people living in rural areas typically go for walks or bike rides in the countryside, while city dwellers might visit leisure centers, playgrounds, or go to football matches. Fishing in rivers or lakes is a popular hobby, too.

Farmers' markets and street food markets are also popular, as is the growing trend for eating out in stylish food halls.

Many Britons also enjoy recreational running and doing a ParkRun, an initiative that began in 2004 in London and is now a global phenomenon. Organized by volunteers, the free 3-mile (5 km) fun run is held every Saturday at 9:00 a.m. in parks around the country, and the activity has a community vibe. Inexperienced and professional runners also challenge themselves to the grueling 26.2-mile (42 km) London Marathon, which has become an annual televised event. Many participants run it in fancy-dress costumes for charity.

DIY and Gardening

The weekend is the time when DIY ("Do It Yourself") and gardening enthusiasts change into their alter egos of craftsmen and artists and begin or continue the process of transforming their homes and gardens. This is an extension of the concept that an "Englishman's home is his castle," and is a wonderful manifestation of an individual's sense of identity, as well as a source of satisfaction and achievement.

Given the fact that home ownership in the UK was 65 percent in 2021—compared, say, to 50 percent in Germany—it is not difficult to understand why the DIY retail sector always prospers when the economy prospers. The industry is led by nationwide hardware chain stores and is given a further boost by TV makeover programs.

Men and women, young and old, enjoy the quintessentially English pastime of gardening throughout the seasons. The annual amount of money spent on garden-related products is considerably greater than that spent on DIY. Gardening books, magazines, and programs on radio and television are a major part of Britain's culture. BBC Radio 4's "Gardeners' Question Time" is the longest-running program of its kind, dating back to 1947.

Britain has many stately homes, parks, and gardens that are open to visitors. Likewise, the National Gardens Scheme opens thousands of gardens in England and Wales to the public on certain days to raise money for nursing and caring charities.

MONEY

These days, it's most likely that Britons will pay for that bottle with a debit card. As the most common method of payment, debit cards accounted for 48 percent of all payments in 2021, according to the banking and finance body UK Finance. Cash remains the second-most popular method of payment, but it has been declining since 2011.

Contactless payments are on the rise, and nearly a third of all payments in the UK were made by contactless cards, cell phones (mobiles), or watches in 2021—a 36 percent increase compared with 2020. This was due to an increase in the contactless payment limit to £100 in 2021, the imposition of social distancing during the Covid-19 pandemic, and more smaller businesses accepting contactless payments. UK Finance predicts that cash will account for only 6 percent of all payments in the UK by 2031.

However, there is a concern that a "cashless society" discriminates against tourists, the elderly, people with disabilities, people who don't have a bank account, and those on low incomes who find budgeting easier with cash.

EVERYDAY SHOPPING

Most people in towns and cities buy food from budget supermarkets such as Lidl, Aldi, Iceland, and Asda. Butchers, fishmongers, bakers, and fruit and vegetable markets are usually good value too. Mid-range supermarkets include Tesco, Morrisons, and Sainsbury's, while Waitrose, Marks & Spencer, Wholefoods, and Planet Organic sell premium goods. Most supermarkets also sell medicine and toiletries, although Britons tend to buy those from pharmacies (known here as chemists) such as Boots or health food stores such as Holland & Barrett.

Many villages still have their own "village shop," or general store, which might double as a post office, although these continue to dwindle in number.

Vast out-of-town shopping malls are also a feature of modern life, although you need a car to get to most of them. Among the best known are Westfield London and Westfield Stratford in the capital, the Metrocentre in Tyne and Wear, the Trafford Centre in Manchester, and Bluewater in Kent.

With the advent of online stores such as Amazon, Asos, and Ocado, it's fair to say that Britain has experienced a shopping revolution. The Covid-19 lockdowns of 2020 saw ecommerce sales jump to 47 percent, and in 2022 online sales accounted for 27 percent of all retail sales in the UK—double the amount of 2012. Buying clothes and electronics online is particularly popular.

In recent years it has become common for people, particularly women, to rent clothes rather than buy them, mostly via websites such as the Hurr Collective, which stocks 65 fashion items to rent.

The popularity of ecommerce, retail parks on the edge of towns, and the inability of independent businesses to compete with chains such as Argos, Poundland, and Primark, has caused Britain's high streets to decline. Some historic nationwide chains haven't even survived, with British Home Stores closing in 2016 and menswear retailer T M Lewin becoming an online business only. This is a problem for the elderly and people without access to the internet. Today, many high streets have a proliferation of cell (mobile) phone shops, coffee shops such as Costa Coffee, Starbucks, and Pret a Manger, and charity shops—although some people welcome the latter, along with car boot sales and flea markets, because they encourage recycling and help reduce landfill.

Market towns with a large number of independent businesses are highly valued, with Treorchy in Mid Glamorgan winning a Great British High Street award. Farmers' markets such as Borough Market in London, antiques markets such as Newark Antiques Fair in Nottinghamshire, and markets selling handmade crafts and produce such as Treacle Market in Macclesfield, Cheshire, are also prized.

FOOD AND DRINK

Pay no attention to the stereotype: British food is tasty and varied. Britain's seas are stocked with fish, while its fertile land and temperate climate, highly suitable for agriculture and livestock, yield fine-quality meat, game, cereal crops, fruits, and vegetables. An abundance of milk and cream meanwhile has given rise to a nation of cheesemakers who rival their counterparts in neighboring France. In the seventeenth century, explorers, traders, and slave plantation owners introduced exotic and unfamiliar produce to Britain, from tea, coffee, and sugar to spices, oranges, bananas, and pineapples.

Pass the roast beef!

Traditional English dishes include soups, stews such as Lancashire hotpot, shepherd's pie (made with lamb), cottage pie (made with beef), and steak and kidney pie. Roast meat, poultry, or game meanwhile is traditionally served with vegetables and a savory baked batter called Yorkshire pudding, accompanied by mustard, horseradish, or gravy. Classic desserts include fruit pies, crumbles, or a cheeseboard with chutney. British beer, cider, and "Scotch" (Scottish malted whisky) are well known for their quality.

The First and Second World Wars, and the years of austerity immediately following them, had a considerable impact on food choices. Most people had to "make do" with whatever they could get, or grow their own. The catchphrase "Dig for Victory" was widely used to encourage people to be as self-sufficient as possible. King George VI even turned some of Buckingham Palace's flowerbeds into vegetable plots. As a result, British people became accustomed to second best for a while—which helps explain the outdated view that British cuisine is mediocre or bland.

Today, cooking contests, such as "Masterchef" and "The Great British Bake-Off," make primetime TV; chefs Jamie Oliver, Gordon Ramsay, Delia Smith, and Nigella Lawson are household names, and companies such as HelloFresh have developed meal kits that are delivered to homes to help people cook.

Home Comfort

Britain's infamous brown sauce, HP Sauce, was registered by a Nottingham grocer in 1895, but today it is manufactured by Heinz in the Netherlands. Made from malt, tomatoes, molasses, and vinegar, it has a ketchup-like consistency. While sales may be falling, the company must be doing something right—because the sauce is honored by a Royal Warrant!

Fish and chips.

Fish and chips—hot, thickly cut fried potatoes served with mushy peas and battered cod, haddock, or plaice—is Britain's national dish. It's often eaten with salt and vinegar, tomato or brown sauce, lemon, and in more recent times, gravy, curry sauce, or cheese. Fish-and-chip shops, or "chippies," first appeared in the 1860s, and expanded rapidly, thanks to the trawlers that hauled in quantities of fish from the North Atlantic and the waters around Norway and Iceland.

Established in 1913, The National Federation of Fish Friers estimates there are 10,500 specialist fish-and-chip shops in the UK. Eighty percent of the population eat the dish once a year, while 22 percent eat it once a week. However, soaring energy bills, depleted fish stocks, a rise in veganism, and greater choice is affecting the industry. Takeout portions of fish and chips used to be wrapped in newspaper until hygiene laws in the 1980s insisted on approved paper boxes.

Meals of the Day

A "full English breakfast" typically consists of some or all of the following, most of which are fried or grilled: eggs, bacon, sausages, potatoes, tomatoes, mushrooms, kidneys, black pudding, baked beans, toast and butter, and tomato ketchup or brown sauce. This is followed by more toast, jam or marmalade, and tea or coffee. While some Britons still make it on weekends, it's also common to enjoy it as an occasional treat in a hotel, guesthouse, or café. Porridge or cereal, eggs cooked in any way, ham, smoked fish such as kippers (smoked herrings), or kedgeree—a dish consisting of rice, smoked haddock, and hard-boiled egg inspired by the British colonial period in India—are also traditional options that are still popular.

These days, however, most people prefer a quicker, lighter meal such as cereal or toast eaten with jam, marmalade, honey, peanut butter, or Marmite—a salty yeast-extract spread. Not to everyone's liking, it is sold with the slogan, "Love it or Hate it." City dwellers might grab a croissant and coffee from a chain café on their way to work. Brunch, a late morning meal combining breakfast and lunch, is saved for lazy weekends.

Lunch for working people during the week tends to be soup, a sandwich, or a salad. A traditional Sunday lunch consists of roast beef, pork, lamb, or chicken, accompanied by potatoes, vegetables, and gravy made from the meat juices or from an instant mix. Desserts, or puddings, were traditionally a fruit tart or bread-and-butter pudding drenched in cream or custard, made from eggs, sugar, milk, and vanilla. More contemporary desserts might be a shop-bought yogurt or cheesecake.

Supper or, in the north, "tea," is a simple family meal eaten at any time in the evening that is convenient. During the week it may consist of a cooked dish, such as lamb chops, cottage pie (minced meat is the main ingredient, topped with mashed potatoes and cooked in the oven), or, these days, pizza or pasta, followed by cheese and fruit. If there is more time to spend on preparation, supper may be a more elaborate meal, but the name implies informality.

You may be invited to dinner, a more formal evening meal, usually accompanied by wine, at 7:30 or 8:00 p.m.

VACATIONS

The average vacation entitlement is twenty working days—this excludes teachers, who get more—plus the standard public holidays, although many companies offer twenty-five days or more. Most companies allow employees to take a maximum of two consecutive weeks, unless a longer period is agreed with the employer beforehand. Britain also tends to close down for a fortnight over the Christmas and New Year period.

Most Britons go away on a two-week vacation during the school summer holidays. People on a budget might choose to camp, sleep in a trailer (a static caravan) on a caravan site, or stay at Butlin's, a chain of affordable seaside resorts, launched in the 1930s.

Bed and breakfasts, where you stay in someone's home, eat a homemade breakfast, and chat with your host, are also common, particularly by the sea. This

Busy beach in summer at Tenby, Pembrokeshire.

became very popular after Airbnb launched in the UK in 2009, with 8.4 million guests choosing to travel this way in the UK between 2017 and 2018. However, critics argue that the business model limits availability for local long-term renters, weakens a destination's sense of community, and drives up rents.

Most Britons chase the sun. If the weather cooperates, they might visit a coastal town such as Blackpool, Anglesey, or Margate to sunbathe, swim in the sea, play on arcade games, and have nights out.

If staying in Britain, the middle classes might invest in a beach hut—although the most sought-after ones now cost around £325,000, the same price as an average house. But it's most likely they'll treat themselves to a rural spa hotel, a boutique hotel in the Cotswolds, or a yachting holiday in the Norfolk Broads. The middle classes typically have several vacations and weekends away a year, perhaps exploring Cornwall's fishing villages and independent art galleries, a vineyard in France, or UNESCO World Heritage Sites in Greece, Florida, or Australia.

The upper classes meanwhile might stay in an all-inclusive resort in the Maldives, go on safari in Tanzania, or cruise around Antarctica.

It's common for middle-class students to take a gap year—a year off from their studies before or after university—to backpack around Southeast Asia or South America, or to travel by Interrail around Europe. Older or wealthier people with a bigger budget may do the same, swapping hostels for hotels in what is dubbed as "flashpacking." Combining a vacation with remote working is also increasingly common, particularly since hybrid working went mainstream following Covid-19.

GIFT GIVING

As we've seen, when invited for a meal it is customary to bring your hosts flowers, chocolates, or a bottle of wine. It's also usual to bring presents for friends, family, and coworkers from exotic lands. Birthdays are occasions for presents and parties. Younger people tend to be more spontaneous in gift giving and, among friends, exchange presents and cards for birthdays and other occasions more often than their parents do. Mothering Sunday (Mother's Day) in March and Father's Day in June have become annual landmarks for families: most children will send a card to each parent, often accompanied by flowers for Mothering Sunday.

CHAPTER SEVEN

TIME OUT

London is a cultural powerhouse. Its music, arts, and theater options are legendary. In addition to world-famous museums and galleries, it is home to many less well-known specialist museums such as the Design Museum, the London Transport Museum, the Imperial War Museum, and the National Maritime Museum—all of which are free to enter. Visitors should book ahead to secure tickets for the opening week of the latest paid-for exhibition or to ensure the best theater seats.

Beyond the capital, there is a wealth of heritage, arts, and history to discover in the main metropolitan centers and regions, including the Eden Project in Cornwall; Portsmouth Historic Dockyard, which displays Nelson's flagship "Victory" from the 1805 Battle of Trafalgar; Kelvingrove Art Gallery and Museum, Glasgow; the Ashmolean Museum, Oxford; Titanic Belfast; and Shakespeare's Birthplace, Stratford-upon-Avon. Information is available from the regional tourist boards.

DINING OUT

It would be an understatement to say that postwar Britain was not a foodie destination. While the oldest restaurants, such as Wilton's, Simpson's Tavern, and Rules, opened in London in the 1700s, ordinary people didn't begin dining out for pleasure until the 1960s or '70s, after they'd discovered new flavors and ingredients on their overseas travels. Their experiences abroad of different cultures and cuisines made them want to eat out more, and they demanded quality. Gradually, more restaurants opened in the cities, and with added competition the restaurant scene was transformed. Today you can find every kind of cuisine in London.

Dress Code

High-end restaurants, events such as polo matches or trade shows, and some luxury hotels expect diners to wear smart, elegant but casual clothing—a dress or trousers and a shirt, shoes rather than sneakers, no sportswear, and nothing ripped, dirty, or creased. However, some more formal establishments such as The Palm Court or The Ritz Restaurant and Terrace in the Ritz Hotel, London, insist on a jacket and tie. Equally, if you are attending the Royal Regatta at Henley on the first weekend of July, particularly if you are a member of the exclusive Leander Rowing Club, dress protocol demands that you wear an appropriate shirt and tie.

Usually, invitations to a formal occasion make the dress code clear. Lounge suit, or "black tie," means dinner jacket (a tuxedo) or a smart dress.

SERVICE AND TIPPING

The British don't like serving others: it is seen as demeaning, and traditionally hospitality was poorly paid. Before Brexit, most waitstaff in the cities were from the EU and as so many left the country after 2016, many restaurants and bars are short-staffed—so service can be a mixed bag. However, since Brexit hospitality staff have received a 10 percent pay rise.

It is common practice to leave a tip of at least 10 percent for taxi drivers, waitstaff, hairdressers, and barbers. Sometimes an optional "service" charge is added to the bill, which solves the problem if you are not sure whether to leave a tip, or how much.

CULTURE AND THE PERFORMING ARTS

A Cultural Cornucopia

When it comes to cultural events, Britain shines, and many of its best-loved events date back centuries.

The Summer Exhibition, held at the Royal Academy in London, was founded in 1769, making it one of Britain's longest-established cultural events. Every June, it gives the public the chance to discover work by up-and-coming artists and household names.

Compared to the Royal Academy's Summer Exhibition, the classical music festival known as The

The Royal Albert Hall, home to the BBC Proms, an eight-week season of classical music concerts.

Proms—established in 1895—is a relative newcomer. Concerts take place between July and September in the Royal Albert Hall. During the grand finale known as "the last night of the Proms," the audience dress up, wave Union Jack flags, and sing "Land of Hope and Glory."

As its name suggests, the Royal Horticultural Society Chelsea Flower Show has attracted members of the royal family since it was founded in 1913. Show gardens and floral displays, talks, and gardening demonstrations take place every May in the grounds of the Royal Hospital in Chelsea, a historic retirement home for army veterans.

Glyndebourne Festival in Sussex meanwhile has been impressing opera fans every summer since 1934.

The Edinburgh Festival in August is a world-renowned platform for all aspects of the performing arts; the open-access Fringe, comprising hundreds of separate (often small) productions, is an entertainment kaleidoscope covering the sublime to the ridiculous.

The Scots are also proud to celebrate the Royal Edinburgh Military Tattoo, which sees military bands, dances, and piping performances take place on the esplanade at Edinburgh Castle in August.

Founded in 1822, the iconic Royal Highland Show is held in June. It showcases Scottish farming, livestock, produce, rural crafts, and different musical bands.

The National Eisteddfod of Wales, established in 1861, is Wales' premiere cultural event. Poetry readings, live music, Welsh cooking demonstrations, and Welsh language lessons take place across Wales every August. The Royal Welsh Show dates back to 1904. Every July, it celebrates agricultural life with sheepdog trials, motorbike stunt displays, and horticultural demonstrations in Llanelwedd, Powys.

Hay Festival, established in 1987, has been described as "the Woodstock of the mind." Held every June in the market town of Hay-on-Wye, this prominent literary festival draws international authors for talks, book signings, and live music.

Museums

London's not-for-profit, permanent public museums are world leaders in researching, collecting, and conserving exhibits for the purposes of education and enjoyment. The British Museum, founded in 1753, was the first national museum to embrace all fields of human knowledge. In terms of visitor numbers, it ranked fourth in the world in

2022, even though museums were still recovering from the Covid-19 lockdown. The Natural History Museum, housed in a late-nineteenth-century neo-Gothic building, ranked third. Meanwhile the fine and applied arts Victoria and Albert Museum (the V&A) had 2.4 million visitors in 2022, and the Science Museum 2.3 million. International visitors also flock to The Royal Observatory in the capital. Founded in 1675 by Charles II, it is home to the Greenwich Meridian line (zero degrees longitude), which determines Greenwich Mean Time.

Beyond London, there is a wealth of knowledge to discover at the Roman Baths and Pump Room in Somerset, Beamish Museum in County Durham, and the Ashmolean Museum in Oxfordshire.

Giant blue whale skeleton in the main hall of the Natural History Museum.

The National Museum of Scotland drew the most visitors in Scotland, with 2 million in 2022. Glasgow's Riverside Museum, Kelvingrove Art Gallery and Museum, and The Burrell Collection—Art Fund Museum of the Year in 2023—are also worth a mention.

For Welsh heritage and culture, Cardiff Castle and the National Museum Cardiff offer a broad overview.

There is a long-standing debate about whether British museums should return certain permanent exhibits to their countries of origin, as many were taken by colonialists in the days of Empire.

Galleries

Like its museums, many of Britain's major art galleries are free to enter. The Tate Modern saw the most visitors in 2022, with 3.9 million. Housed in a huge former power station, this gallery of contemporary and modern art expanded its collection with an extension in 2016. Its neighbor, the Southbank Centre—a vast cultural complex consisting of the Hayward Gallery and performance spaces such as the Royal Festival Hall and Queen Elizabeth Hall—attracted 2.9 million visitors, followed by the National Gallery (2.7 million) in Trafalgar Square, whose permanent art collection dates back to 1824.

In Scotland, 1.3 million visitors browsed the Scottish National Gallery's collection, which opened to the public in 1859. Art connoisseurs in Wales meanwhile may wish to visit the National Museum of Art in Cardiff and Swansea's Glynn Vivian Art Gallery, a partner of London's Tate. Wales is also planning to create a National Contemporary Art Gallery.

The extension to the Serpentine North Gallery in Hyde Park, designed by Zaha Hadid.

Individual exhibitions and works may draw crowds, but newer galleries have the power to regenerate entire towns. Towner Eastbourne, Margate's Turner Contemporary, and Hastings Contemporary have helped revitalize the south coast in recent years, while The Mining Art Gallery, which opened in 2017, has had a positive impact on County Durham.

Theater

Theater in Britain has deep roots, a vibrant tradition, and today is a trailblazer in modern and experimental productions. "Theatreland" in London's West End is renowned for the range and quality of its plays and musicals and is home to forty theaters. Its longest-running show, Agatha Christie's *The Mousetrap*, took to the stage in 1952—audiences are traditionally asked not to reveal the ending. *Les Misérables, The Phantom of*

The Garrick Theatre in London's Charing Cross Road.

the Opera, and *The Woman in Black* have all been running since the 1980s. Book well in advance to ensure you don't miss out, particularly if a celebrity is playing a leading role. The Southbank Centre on the Thames is home to the National Theatre, and The Royal Shakespeare Company is based in Stratford-upon-Avon in Warwickshire. There are regional theaters across the country, such as the Chichester Festival Theater in West Sussex.

The British love of spectacle and language continues to find expression in local amateur dramatic society productions, pantomimes held over Christmas, and variety shows with comedians, singers, and magicians, which are held in summer in seaside towns such as Blackpool. Stand-up comedy is also popular, thanks to Britain's freedom of speech laws, although recently there have been calls by some to "cancel" comedians whose jokes are considered offensive.

The Music Scene

London is the epicenter of classical music making, with four symphony orchestras and many chamber orchestras and choirs. Venues include the Royal Albert Hall, the Royal Festival Hall, Wigmore Hall, the Barbican Centre, Cadogan Hall, and King's Place. There are also lunchtime concerts at affordable prices in churches such as St. Martin in the Fields. Other distinguished national venues include The Bridgewater Hall in Manchester, The Usher Hall in Edinburgh, and Belfast's Waterfront Hall.

The Royal Opera House in London's Covent Garden area was built in 1858 on the site of a much older theater. Elsewhere, opera fans can watch pop-up

The Royal Opera House with Enzo Plazzotta's statue of a young dancer in the foreground.

performances across Scotland by the Scottish Opera or listen to the Northern Ireland Opera at the Grand Opera House in Belfast. The Welsh National Opera, which was founded in 1943, is based at the contemporary Wales Millennium Center in Cardiff.

Britain's Royal Ballet is one of the most famous classical ballet companies in the world. Based at the Royal Opera House, it is the largest of the five major ballet companies in the country. The contemporary dance company Rambert is based at Sadler's Wells theater in Islington. This venue began life as a music house in 1683, and today it commissions blockbuster performances, groundbreaking new works, hosts dance workshops, and supports emerging dancers and choreographers. Other notable companies are the English National Ballet, founded in 1950, and the Scottish Ballet formed in 1969, which is based in Glasgow. Its Welsh counterpart, Ballet Cymru, was established in 1986.

Chart Music

London, Manchester, Liverpool, and Glasgow are all known for their live music scenes, with venues ranging from the 90,000-seat Wembley Stadium in London to the more intimate Cavern Club in Liverpool where the Beatles played, and Glasgow's legendary live music venue and bar, King Tut's Wah Wah Hut.

British creativity has led to the development of new musical genres. Britpop, a form of alternative rock characterized by regional British accents and cultural references, emerged in the mid-1990s, with bands such as Oasis, Blur, Suede, and Pulp leading the way. Around the same time, garage—a form of electronic dance music—developed in England. Inspired by jungle, house, and R&B, the Artful Dodger and Craig David were at the forefront of the scene. Grime was also inspired by jungle and hip hop. Recognizable for its fast beats and lyrics about gritty urban life, the genre emerged in London in the early 2000s. The artists Stormzy and Dizzee Rascal are most closely associated with the style.

A-list stars, top-of-the-range sound systems, and a chance to bond, run wild, and see multiple artists ensure that music festivals continue to be popular. The biggest, Glastonbury, started in 1970 and now attracts 210,000 people, transforming a farm in Somerset into a pop-up city. Southern England also hosts the Isle of Wight Festival and British Summer Time in London, with headliners such as Elton John. Other popular festivals include the Reading and Leeds Festivals, Parklife in Manchester, and Creamfields, a dance, house, and techno festival in Cheshire.

Established in 1978, the Edinburgh Jazz & Blues Festival is still going strong while the Shetland Folk Festival has been going since 1981. In Wales the Green Man Festival in Powys attracts up to 25,000 visitors.

Combining spectacle and music, London's famous Notting Hill Carnival in August is the largest celebration of Caribbean music and culture in Europe.

Cinema

The British film scene centers on London, with film studios in the capital, in Greater London, and the home counties around it. Once it completes its

Samba drummers at the Notting Hill Carnival in London.

expansion, Shepperton Studios in Surrey—which is behind *Gladiator*, *Billy Elliot*, and *Love Actually*—will become the world's second-largest studio after India's Ramoji Film City. For now though, Pinewood Studios in Buckinghamshire, which dates back to the 1930s, is the largest. The most well known, however, is Studios Leavesden in Hertfordshire, thanks to its Warner Bros. Studio Tour – The Making of Harry Potter. FirstStage Studios in Edinburgh is among the newest, having opened in 2020. London's Soho is the epicenter of Britain's post-production industry.

While on-demand services have seen a decline in the number of British cinemas, there has been an increase in the number of cinemas built in new apartment buildings and in cinemas offering sofas, double beds, sophisticated meals, and cocktails delivered to your seat.

Film fans can watch blockbusters at multiplexes such as the Odeon, Vue, and Cineworld, or at independent boutique cinemas such as The Curzon, Picturehouse, or the Everyman. The British Film Institute's BFI

Southbank in London is a repertory cinema showing world cinema, documentaries, and exhibitions while hosting premieres and talks.

SPORTS

Several of the world's great games were invented in this country—including cricket, tennis, and football—and whether you are a player or a spectator, Britain is a sporting heaven.

Football

Football (US, soccer) is Britain's national sport and has even been described as a "new religion." The industry is driven by the multimillion-pound clubs of the Premier League, dominated by Arsenal, Chelsea, Everton, Liverpool, Manchester United, and Tottenham Hotspur, which opened a new stadium in north London in 2019.

Historically, football was associated with the working classes and blighted by hooliganism; today it attracts a broad audience. More women and families watch and play the game these days, and a generation of female footballers has been inspired by the 2002 film *Bend It Like Beckham* and by the inclusivity of the 2012 Summer Olympics and Paralympics in London. This cultural shift has led to successes such as the British Lionesses winning the 2022 European Championships and reaching the final of the FIFA Women's World Cup in 2023.

Rugby

The modern form of rugby, originally referred to as rugby football, is believed to have started at Rugby School in Warwickshire in 1823, although this is disputed. Whether true or not, it is still considered a sport for the middle classes and is typically played at boys' private schools.

There are two types of rugby: Rugby Union and Rugby League, which have different rules, for example, for scoring and possession. Rugby Union was formed in 1871 and its rules are used in major tournaments such as the World Cup and Six Nations—an annual championship between England, Scotland, Wales, Ireland, France, and Italy—so it's often considered to be the "true" form of the game. There are fifteen players in a team and eight substitutes are allowed during a game. It uses a larger pitch than Rugby League, which has thirteen players a side and allows up to ten substitutes.

As with football, more women are playing rugby, and women's teams are attracting bigger crowds thanks largely to increased TV coverage.

Cricket

Cricket is thought to have been invented in southern England in Saxon or Norman times, and since the 1600s British traders and settlers have spread it around the world. Today it's generally associated with the middle classes and rural life, although city dwellers can also watch matches at Lord's (home of the MCC, Marylebone Cricket Club) and The Oval cricket grounds in London.

A match can take up to a whole day to complete, or, in the case of Test Cricket, up to five days. Self-evidently, it is a serious game that requires endurance, commitment, and application. Everybody in the team takes part batting or fielding—and for some, bowling—and usually everybody gets the chance to hit the ball and score runs.

Golf and Other Sports

Another great British sport, golf, originated in Scotland in the mid-1400s, and King James IV of Scotland was a fan. The first 18-hole course was created in 1764 in the town of St. Andrews, establishing the game as we know it today. In 2017, there were 1,872 courses in England, 560 in Scotland, and 145 in Wales. Colin Montgomerie, Justin Rose, and Nick Faldo are considered to be some of Britain's greatest golfers.

A cricket match on a summer's day.

MAIN SPORTING EVENTS

February and March: Six Nations Rugby, Wales

March: The Boat Race, Southwest London

May: The Horse Trials at Badminton, Badminton House, Gloucestershire

May: Highland Games, Scotland

June: Derby Day, Epsom, Surrey

July: Royal Ascot, Ascot, Berkshire

June–July: Wimbledon, London

July: Henley Regatta, Henley-on-Thames, Oxfordshire

August: Cowes Week, Isle of Wight

Horseback riding is also a popular pastime. The Pony Club, the international youth organization, has some 50,000 members in the UK, while the British Riding Club has 34,000. Professional riders compete in racing events that are held throughout the year. The biggest, the Grand National, takes place in April at Aintree, Liverpool. It is a punishing test of endurance for young horses and their riders, who are often unknown, and vast numbers of the population who otherwise would never be seen in a betting shop enjoy placing "one-off" bets on the winner. The race takes place over a 2.25-mile (3,600 m) circuit, run twice, comprising thirty fences. Royal Ascot in June attracts royalty and media interest, so it is also a famous society fashion occasion, at which women show off their clothes, especially their hats.

SHOPPING FOR PLEASURE

Visitors will find iconic global brands, independent family-run boutiques, and historical shops with original décor across the country.

Tourists flock to London's famous department stores such as Harrods in Knightsbridge, Liberty's, or Hamleys toy shop on Regent Street, and Fortnum & Mason on Piccadilly, which is patronized by the Royal Family. The rich and famous also shop in historic arcades in Mayfair and St. James and at tailors in Saville Row. Elsewhere, visitors are drawn to classic shops in Birmingham's Jewellery Quarter, Queen's Arcade

The elegant, upmarket Burlington Arcade off London's Piccadilly.

in Belfast, and Glasgow's "Style Mile" along Argyle, Buchanan, and Sauchiehall Streets.

If you'd like to buy a classic British souvenir, consider Scotch whisky or finely woven woolen goods such as kilts; Welsh tapestry, slate coasters, or Welsh cakes; or Liberty fabric, English gin, or Wedgwood fine china.

By Royal Appointment

Since medieval times, official suppliers of goods and services to the royal family have received recognition from the monarch. Today, around 800 businesses have applied for a royal warrant, which permits them to display a sign that they are "By Royal Appointment . . ." for five years. Holders include the Welsh cheesemonger Caws Cenarth Cheese, the Scottish jewelers Hamilton & Inches, and the London wine merchant Berry Bros & Rudd, established in 1698.

Antiques and Flea Markets

All British cities and many towns have regular antiques fairs, flea markets, and car boot sales that sell antique silver, furniture, paintings, and second-hand books among the bric-a-brac. Television programs such as the BBC's "Antiques Roadshow" are hugely popular.

CHAPTER EIGHT

TRAVEL, HEALTH, & SAFETY

INTERCITY TRAVEL

Britain has a reasonable public transportation system. Everybody complains about it, but it's safe, clean, and usually reliable. The cheapest way to travel long distance is by bus (coach). National Express runs scheduled, nationwide coach services, and there are many other bus services operating around the country. Some long-distance coaches have toilets on board and most stop at expressway service stations, such as Welcome Break, so passengers can use the toilets or buy hot drinks, meals, snacks, and magazines.

Trains are faster, of course, but expensive, and sometimes cancelled because of strikes or delayed because of signal failure, trespassers, wet weather, and even too many leaves on the track. If your train is delayed, you may be able to claim compensation. National Rail's website provides further information.

Britain's first domestic high-speed railway (known as HS1) runs up to 140 mph (225 kmph) on the 67-mile (108 km) link from the Channel Tunnel at Folkestone to St. Pancras station in London. It uses the railway built for the Eurostar high-speed service to Paris and Brussels. A second, controversial, high-speed railway (HS2) is planned from Euston (a short walk from St. Pancras) to Birmingham.

While people in northern Britain have a reputation for being friendlier than southerners, most people avoid talking to strangers on public transportation. Talking on a cell phone is common, but it's considered polite to keep conversations quiet to avoid disturbing others. Most trains have a quiet carriage where passengers are not allowed to use cell phones.

Driving

In Britain, you drive on the left. Roads are generally good, even though economic hardship has affected road maintenance budgets. There's a nationwide network of expressways, called motorways, designated by the letter M; for example, the M1 runs from north London to near Leeds. Smaller A and B roads are usually slower but more scenic. Some rural roads are little more than winding tracks and you'll need to pull over to allow another vehicle to pass.

The national speed limits are 70 mph (113 kmph) on motorways, 60 mph (97 kmph) on open roads, 40 mph (64 kmph) on dual carriageways often on the outskirts of towns, and 30 mph (48 kmph) within towns (in some cases 20 mph, or 32 kmph). Police or speed cameras might catch you speeding, which will result in a verbal warning or a fine. Unlike in some countries, it is illegal to drive while holding a cell phone or to do a U-turn at traffic signals. It is the driver's responsibility to ensure all passengers are wearing a seatbelt. At gas stations drivers fill up their vehicles with fuel themselves.

When traveling around Britain, it is a good idea to go to the local tourist information offices. They can help with places to stay, travel advice, and suggestions for what to see and do in the area.

URBAN TRANSPORTATION

Many cities have extensive bus, train, and streetcar (or tram) networks, for example, Manchester, Nottingham, and Edinburgh. Most also provide bicycles to hire, and more recently e-bikes and e-scooters, which you pay

Regent Street at night, with the entrance to Piccadilly Circus underground station.

to use temporarily, usually through an app. Some brands such as Lime allow users to leave the e-bike or e-scooter anywhere they like once they've finished with it. This has caused issues, particularly for people who are partially sighted, in a wheelchair, or using a stroller.

In London, in addition to the underground railway system known as the Tube, there are black cabs (taxis), single- and double-decker buses, overground rail services, and the hybrid urban–suburban Elizabeth railway line, which opened in 2022. The 73-mile (117 km) route through the London region runs from Reading, west of the capital, via London Heathrow airport, through the city, to Shenfield and Abbey Wood to the east.

There is a modern tram network in Birmingham, Britain's second-largest city.

The standard, and most economical, method of payment for public transportation in London is a contactless smart card called an Oyster card, which can be used on different modes of travel, including London Buses, London Underground, the Docklands Light Railway (DLR), London Overground, Tramlink, some river boat services, and most National Rail services within the London fare zones. Public transportation services are less frequent, or may stop altogether, on Sundays, public holidays, and at night.

Drivers must pay a congestion charge to enter central London at busy times, while older vehicles are subject to an Ultra Low Emission Zone (ULEZ) charge to help keep London's air clean.

HEALTH

Foreign visitors on vacation or doing business in Britain are not required to have travel or health insurance, and as the National Health Service is free at the point of delivery no one will ask you whether or not you've got it. You may, however, be charged depending on your legal status in the country. A&E is free for everybody. However, it's a good idea to take out a policy before your departure to ensure that you're covered for all eventualities, including repatriation or emergency dental work.

Britain doesn't require visitors to have any vaccinations before arriving in the country. If you are resident here and you need a vaccination for a vacation abroad, you can ask your NHS doctor or pay for it at a private travel clinic such as Nomad Travel.

For free 24-hour healthcare advice, the phone number is 111; the phone number for emergency services (police, ambulance, fire, and coastguard) is 999.

SAFETY

Is Britain safe? Safety is relative, but overall, most visitors who take sensible precautions needn't worry about their safety. There are no great natural hazards or dangerous animals. Britain doesn't suffer from hurricanes, and tsunamis are unlikely. Earthquakes, cyclones, and tornadoes do occur, but these are rare and don't usually cause serious damage. Flooding is the most common natural disaster, particularly around rivers and low-lying coastal areas.

The UK has strict gun laws, so while gun crime is rising it is still low, and is usually related to organized crime such as gangs or county lines—criminal networks which coerce or encourage usually children or vulnerable people to carry illegal drugs across police or local authority boundaries. Knife crime is more prevalent, particularly in the West Midlands.

Domestic violence and rape most commonly affect women. According to the charity Rape Crisis, one in four women in England and Wales have experienced rape or sexual assault. Conviction rates for rape are very low.

You can help to stay safe with common sense precautions. Cover your legs when walking in long grass to avoid tick bites. Avoid coastal promenades in storms, and unlit areas at night. Consider carrying an attack alarm, and never leave your drink unattended in a pub, bar, or club; make sure your valuables are zipped up in a bag that's not easy to grab to deter pickpockets; use only licensed taxis, and lock windows and doors when you leave the place you're staying at. If you're staying in a hotel with a safe, store your passport in that unless you think you'll need it for ID to access a nightclub, or to buy alcohol.

In an emergency shout for help and call 999 for the emergency services—an ambulance, the fire brigade, police, or coastguard. There are around 100,000 public defibrillators in gyms, malls, community centers, and elsewhere, if needed.

CHAPTER NINE

BUSINESS BRIEFING

After the Second World War the British economy was devastated and had to adapt to a changed reality. The loss of its captive imperial market and the gradual decline of its industrial and manufacturing base led to a switch to financial services. One lasting legacy of the empire was the emergence of the City of London as one of the world's major financial hubs.

Napoleon once dismissed the British as "a nation of shopkeepers." A shopkeeper's daughter, Margaret Thatcher, dramatically transformed Britain's postwar business landscape. She believed in the power of free markets, in limiting government spending, and in cutting taxes to encourage and reward entrepreneurship. The result was a wholesale deregulation of the economy, privatization of key national industries, the marginalizing of trade unions to keep the workforce flexible, and the centralizing of power from local authorities to central government. Many traditional assumptions, social structures, and ways of life and working were swept aside. These radical reforms were brutal but effective and led to the rise of a new breed of driven businesspeople nicknamed "yuppies" (young urban professionals). The twenty-first century, however, has witnessed new challenges to global and domestic stability. Britain's business environment today has been buffeted by the fallout from the 2008 international banking crisis, the unfolding effects of Brexit, changes in working patterns brought about by the Covid-19 lockdown, made possible by the exponential growth of new technology, social media and AI, and the rising cost and uncertainty caused by armed conflicts in Ukraine and elsewhere.

THE NEW WORKING CULTURE

Most British offices today are open plan, and since 2007 they have all been non-smoking spaces. Office life has also been transformed by the trend for coworking spaces—a single building, floor, or room that accommodates people from different companies. Such spaces are particularly popular with startups and freelancers, attracted to the business model's flexibility—and often, free beer and ping-pong. In 2020, Coworking Resources partnered with the world's largest coworking listing platform, www.coworker. com, to create a Global Coworking Growth Study. The study revealed hot desking—when employees work from an available desk according to a rota system or

Coworking spaces can be found throughout Britain's major cities.

first-come, first-served basis—has been growing since 2015. The US leads the way, with 3,700 coworking spaces, followed by India (2,197), then the UK, with 1,044—most of which are in London.

The Covid-19 lockdowns of 2020 and 2021, however, led to another revolution: working from home. Within weeks, Britain's office workers were hosting meetings over Zoom, and the popularity of hybrid working—a combination of working from home and an office—remained in 2022 and beyond. However, major employers began to encourage employees back to the office in 2023.

Hip companies attract employees with days off on their birthday, refrigerators stocked with beer, or even gin trolleys. A small number of employers such as NatWest Bank, the law firm Freshfields, energy firm Centrica, and investment service BlackRock have also begun offering discounted fertility treatment, such as egg freezing for women. There is a growing awareness that women experiencing the menopause also require extra support at work.

WOMEN IN BUSINESS

Equal rights for women in the world of work are enshrined in law; but there are areas where the "glass ceiling" continues to inhibit their advancement and equal pay has yet to be achieved. Nevertheless, there are today more women at the top than ever before. Organizations such as the British Association of Women Entrepreneurs and the social enterprise Prowess—formerly the National Association for the Promotion of Women's Enterprise—

Deborah Meaden, one of the investors in the reality TV business program "Dragons' Den."

support women business owners. According to the Office of National Statistics, around 10 percent of women were self-employed compared to 16 percent of men in 2023. This number is growing, with women citing the need for flexibility around childcare as their main reason for starting a business.

TRADE UNIONISM

The reform of trade unionism in the Thatcher years helped to bring about the rebirth of the British economy in the mid-1980s. The prosperity that followed has continued more or less uninterrupted ever since—apart from three major storms the economy had to contend with. First was Britain's sudden withdrawal in 1991 from the European Monetary Union, which caused huge increases in interest rates, resulting in many people losing their homes, and businesses going bust. The second was the fallout from the world financial crisis of 2007–8, followed by the tax and spending policies of the Labour government, which prompted the austerity measures of the incoming coalition government of 2010. The third was the impact of the Covid-19 pandemic.

These experiences have triggered a revival of trade union activism and a hardening of left-of-center positions, resulting in a return to public sector strike action, including teachers, police, hospital staff, the fire and rescue services, and transportation workers across the London Tube, rail, and bus services.

MEETINGS

In most circumstances, you can e-mail or call someone to arrange a meeting, although in some sectors such as law, or when you wish to speak to the CEO of a major corporation, you may need to go through a personal assistant first. If you've requested a virtual meeting, once the day and time have been agreed, send your business contact an agenda and a link via Zoom, Google Meet, or Microsoft Teams, for example.

Being on time for appointments is essential. Don't be late. On the other hand, don't arrive too early. Arriving five minutes before the appointed time is the sweet spot. This rule also holds for virtual meetings and evening arrangements, for example, for dinner at a restaurant. If you are unavoidably held up, call in advance.

An exchange of pleasantries is expected at the start of a meeting; avoid being excessively loud, humorous, polite, or over-familiar.

When you first meet a business contact, and when you say good-bye, you should shake hands. Typical greetings are, "Hello, nice to meet you," or the traditional "How do you do." In responding to a "thank you" it has become common to say, "You're welcome."

When meeting a contact or leaving, you may also be expected to exchange business cards. However, this is less usual these days, with younger people discussing their LinkedIn profile or Instagram handle, or sending each other a quick e-mail with their contact details as a way to keep in touch.

It's now common to use first names when speaking or writing to a business contact, even if you've never met them before. However, when dealing with a very important client or overseas visitor, you may want to take their lead or err on the side of caution and address them as Mr. or Ms with their surname, unless they tell you they're comfortable with your using their first name. If you're not sure if a woman is married, don't use "Mrs."

Recognition of an individual's professional status, such as Dr. (medical or academic doctor), Professor, or rank within the Armed Services, is the required etiquette. In general, beginning an e-mail with "Hi Peter," for example, is widespread; "Dear Peter," or "Hello Peter" are more formal.

Dressing smartly for business meetings is essential. In formal settings such as an investment bank in London's Canary Wharf, this means suits for men, in black, navy, or dark gray, with a tie. Women should wear a smart jacket with trousers or a neat skirt that's not too high above the knee. Personal hygiene and a well-groomed appearance are important. If you like to wear fragrance, a subtle one is best.

Since the 1990s, there has been a movement toward "dressing down"—wearing less formal clothes at work. Before the Covid-19 pandemic this was particularly the case on Fridays. During the pandemic some people took this a step too far, with some workers being caught out wearing pajamas on Zoom meetings.

Friendship in Business

Bear in mind that the British tend to compartmentalize their lives and have a heightened sense of privacy and personal space. This is reinforced by adherence to the old axiom of "never mix business and pleasure"—hence a reticence about making friends in a business context, in the sense of close relationships. People are often aware of the possibility of spoiling a good working relationship by making a presumption of something closer. For many of the younger generation this is no longer the barrier it once was. However, there is a world of difference between being friendly toward someone and assuming that this is real friendship.

PRESENTATIONS

When giving a presentation on PowerPoint, Google Slides, or the like, it's important first to establish your credibility before launching into the pitch. You may catch their attention with a surprising statistic or an inoffensive joke—some humor is acceptable and can help enliven a dry presentation. Let your audience know at the beginning that you will answer questions at the end.

NEGOTIATION STYLES

British negotiation and interview styles are markedly different from those in the US, as Britons tend to be indirect, affable, and relaxed, and, as we've noted, humor is not necessarily out of place. The American approach tends to be shorter, to the point, and much more blunt; individuals sell themselves hard, leaving the other side in no doubt as to their strengths and merits. Pleasantries are typically not exchanged.

Remember, too, in this context that, given the typical British preference for understatement, you may have to exercise great patience in doing business at this level. If it is generally true that Americans like to be "sold" something, it is equally true that the British like to "buy" something, and they can sometimes take a long time to make up their minds. So do not attempt to make a hard sell in Britain. Everything will be understated, and you may well have to probe and even pester in order to determine the value of the product or service that interests you. In other words, as a buyer, you will actually need to ask!

CONTRACTS

British contract law is mainly based on case law, or legal precedents, unlike the codified civil law of the European legal system. Contracts in Britain therefore tend to be much more detailed than in the EU. It is important to read the contract very carefully and query any terms or phrases you don't understand or disagree with—your counterpart, whether prospective boss or client, may be willing to adjust the terms. Once it is signed and dated by both parties it is legally binding and must be followed.

RESOLVING DISPUTES

In the event of a breach of the terms of a contract, such as failure to deliver on time or substandard goods, the best way to resolve matters is to talk to the party or person you disagree with in private in a calm manner. It's a good idea to take note of the date, time, and nature of the conversation in case the dispute escalates. This applies as much to internal workplace disagreements as to company disputes. Litigation is always expensive and time consuming. An alternative option is for both parties to agree to arbitration—a private procedure in which one or more arbitrators make a binding decision on the dispute. This can avoid costly and public court cases.

In the case of a workplace dispute, if the feud continues write to the company's HR department or seek guidance from your trade union if you're a member, or from Citizen's Advice, a free, independent service.

In cases where you believe someone owes you money, you can pay a small fee to apply to a small claims court or sue them by making a civil claim.

BUSINESS GIFTS

Exchanging lavish gifts is not usually expected or done in a British business context, as it may be considered a bribe. Large corporations expect employees to inform their managers when they receive an expensive gift. However, if you give a small present such as food, wine, or craftwork from your country, it will always be welcomed. It's also common practice for a company to treat valued clients to a present at Christmas, such as, for example, a hamper of luxury food and drink.

Branded corporate gifts such as calendars bearing a company logo are common as well. At product launch parties and similar events, guests will usually receive a "goody bag."

THE VALUE OF GOOD MANNERS

The British believe that "manners makyth man," and this applies in business too. Quiet confidence and courtesy will make a positive impression on your business associates.

CHAPTER TEN

COMMUNICATING

The English language has evolved over centuries. Old English is rooted in the North Sea Germanic dialects brought to Britain in the fifth century by the Anglo-Saxons. The Norman Conquest of 1066 infused it with French influences, enriching its grammar and vocabulary, and it absorbed words from Greek and Latin, the languages of scholarship and learning in the Middle Ages. As Britain's Empire expanded English became commonly spoken around the world. A form of soft power, it has fostered cultural exchange and become integral to diplomacy, business, the arts, and communications.

SPOKEN ENGLISH

British history has left a remarkable "voiceprint" across the country. Accents and dialects can differ even within the same region, reflecting the cultural impact of past events. Even when Chaucer was writing *The Canterbury Tales* at the end of the fourteenth century, he was drawing on a Middle English vocabulary that contained Celtic, Classical, Vulgar, and Medieval Latin, Saxon, Jutish, Northumbrian, Norman French, Central French, Danish, and Norwegian. Since then, elements borrowed from the rest of the world have been added—from Hindi and Urdu to African-American rap.

For much of the twentieth century, the BBC and other institutions promoted "received pronunciation," also known as the Queen's English as Queen Elizabeth II spoke in this way. Today, it is recognized that no such standard is necessary, and that regional accents have their own intrinsic value—from the TV presenters Ant and Dec's Tyneside "Geordie" dialect to the singer Adele's London accent. A key difference between northern British accents and southern ones is that the "flat vowel" sound is widely used throughout the north. Words such as "laughter" are therefore pronounced "lafter," to rhyme with "patter," in the north and "laafter," as in "partner," in the south.

BODY LANGUAGE

Overall, the British are less physically expressive than other Europeans such as, say, the Italians. However, some gestures you might come across include mimicking signing your name to ask for the check in a restaurant, crossing the middle finger over the forefinger to wish

ACCENTS AND PHRASES

Can you guess the meaning behind these common regional phrases?

1. Geordie, from Newcastle: Haddaway man!

2. Londoner: He's from my ends, innit?

3. Welsh: That's tidy, that is.

4. Scottish: She's a bonnie lass.

5. Cornish, from Cornwall: I'll finish it dreckly.

6. Mancunian, from Manchester: Stop mithering me.

7. Scouse, from Liverpool: Do you fancy a bevy in that sound new bar?

Answers:

1. You must be joking.

2. He's from my area, isn't he? (Originally a contraction of "isn't it?," "innit" is now commonly tagged on to any sentence to prompt a response).

3. That's great.

4. She's a pretty girl.

5. I'll finish it at some point in the near future.

6. Stop annoying me.

7. Would you like an alcoholic drink in that cool new bar?

someone luck, wobbling an open palm to mean "so-so," and tapping the side of your nose with an index finger to warn others not to be nosy.

A uniquely British gesture is a rather rude one. A Brit "sticks two fingers up" at someone by extending their forefinger and middle finger into a V sign, with their palm faced towards themselves. Legend has it that the gesture dates back to the Battle of Agincourt in 1415, when the French captured British archers and chopped off the two fingers they needed to draw a bowstring. British archers who had not been disfigured taunted the French by showing them their fingers.

The British value their personal space, so it's considered good manners to allow someone to step out of an elevator (or "lift") first, or not get too close to others. In fact, a 2017 survey of 8,943 participants from 42 countries found that Britons prefer to stay thirty-one inches away from acquaintances (compared to thirty for Argentinians) and twenty inches from a close friend (sixteen for Argentinians). If a British person accidentally brushes past someone, they will apologize.

THE MEDIA

Freedom of the press is one of the cornerstones of Britain's democracy, enabling journalists to fact-check, challenge powerful people, organizations, and political parties, and hold them to account. However, while all parties subscribe to this principle, it doesn't mean those in power have to like it—and chances are that Prime Minister Theresa May wasn't so keen on the irreverent gifs that mocked her robotic dance moves in 2018.

In the past, the British public consumed the news from newspapers, television, or radio. Today they are as likely to learn of breaking news from social media. Yet while social media allows stories to break in real time, and gives people a collective voice, a lack of fact-checking has led to an increase in the airing of unsubstantiated claims, or "fake news."

Newspapers

Regional and national newspapers have been in decline for years. With the rise of the internet and social media platforms, most newspapers now also have an online presence. Some websites require readers to register free or pay to access the content (known as a paywall).

The British press can be roughly divided into "quality press," or broadsheets—named for their original larger size—and tabloids, known as the "popular press" or "red tops"—so-called because they have red logos.

Of the broadsheets, *The Guardian/The Observer* are left of center; *The Independent* (online only since 2016) and *i/iWeekend* have a centrist political slant, and *The Times/The Sunday Times*, and *The Financial Times* are center-right. *The Telegraph/The Sunday Telegraph* are right-wing. Educated readers with an interest in politics, current affairs, and economics might also read magazines such as *The Economist*, *Private Eye*, *The Spectator*, *New Statesman*, and *The Week*.

The Sun/The Sun on Sunday and *Express* tabloids are both right-wing, as is the *Daily Mail/The Mail on Sunday*; at the time of writing, the *Daily Mail* was the most popular paid-for newspaper, with a circulation of 746,000.

The *Daily Star/Daily Star Sunday* are also tabloids, focusing more on football, celebrities, and true crime than on politics. The *Daily Mirror/Sunday Mirror* and *Sunday People* are center-left.

Most cities distribute free papers as well, such as the *Evening Standard* and *City A.M.* The *Metro* is the most popular free paper, with a circulation of 952,000.

Televsion

All people pay for an annual TV license, which helps fund services by the British Broadcasting Corporation. Leading terrestrial channels include BBC One, which is globally respected for its news bulletins, current affairs programs, and original dramas, and BBC Two, which is best known for its documentaries. The others include ITV, a commercial network that targets viewers under thirty-five and hosts popular soaps such as "Coronation Street," and Channel 4, whose remit is to commission programs from outside production companies.

Today, on-demand streaming services are tempting viewers, particularly younger viewers, away from terrestrial TV. Netflix is the most subscribed streaming platform worldwide, although Amazon Prime Video, Apple TV+, Disney+, NOW, BritBox, DAZN, and Hayu are also available in the UK. Sky is popular, too, particularly with sports fans.

SERVICES

Telephone

Telephone communication has come a long way since the era of the rotary phone thanks to the rise in cell phones and smartphones in the late 2000s. In 2023,

98 percent of adults aged sixteen to twenty-four in the UK had a smartphone, and USwitch predicts that 95 percent of the UK population will be using a smartphone by 2025. Landline use is in freefall, although the use of cell phones to make calls is also decreasing as they have been replaced by texting.

Mail

Since the Royal Mail was established in 1516, the British postal system has been synonymous with reliability and efficiency. Red letter boxes and postage stamps are emblematic of this venerable institution, which has played such a crucial role in communication and commerce. However, the postal landscape is changing, with electronic communication and alternative delivery services presenting it with challenges. In 2023, Royal Mail's monopoly dissolved when it signed deals with Evri and DPD, marking a transformative shift. As traditional mail faces decline, the British postal system is grappling with the need to reinvent itself in a digital age, navigating changes in consumer preference and emerging competition.

The Internet and Social Media

Internet use is nearly universal. In 2022, according to the communications regulator Ofcom, only 6 percent of UK households had no internet access. Broadband speeds vary, though, with an average of 80 Mbps; rural areas may experience slower connections. Britain is in the process of introducing 5G mobile technology, which will provide speedier connection to the internet and allow more devices to be connected to it in a smaller geographic area.

As with telephone use, Britons—particularly those aged twenty-five to thirty-four—are gradually shunning desktop computers in favor of smartphones or other devices to access the internet.

Online activities range from social media and streaming to gaming, work, and education. The Covid-19 pandemic intensified a general reliance on the internet for remote work and virtual interaction.

On average, British people spend three and a half hours online each day, mostly to send or receive e-mails (85 percent), research goods or services (81 percent), and do internet banking (76 percent). Messaging services, social media, and reading the news also rank highly.

The most popular social media platforms are the US-owned Facebook, Instagram, Snapchat, X, and YouTube. The Chinese-owned TikTok platform, which allows users to create and watch short videos, was banned on UK government devices in 2023 due to national security concerns. Protection from inappropriate or offensive content is a growing concern.

CONCLUSION

These pages have explored many aspects of the complex British character and what it means to be British. Some Britons might argue that the 2014 referendum on

Scottish independence, the 2016 vote for Brexit, and the ongoing but quieter demands for independence from Wales and Cornwall reveal a fragmented nation.

However, as a family of nations, the British also share common traits, such as a delight in creativity, and common values such as a love of the NHS, the monarchy, and the BBC, which, despite recent scandals, remains the world's most respected public broadcaster. There is still an overarching feeling of belonging that gives the country its unique character.

The British capacity for fair-mindedness, tolerance, and compromise (although severely tested) is as strong as ever, and the country continues to produce highly gifted individuals capable of creating a Covid-19 vaccination, establishing a nationwide organ donor register, and creating AI-controlled cameras and microphones to identify and monitor wildlife.

The British people continue to be courteous but stubborn, funny but infuriating, friendly but slow to make friends. Britain remains a remarkable and fascinating conundrum—to itself as well as to the outside world.

USEFUL APPS

Communication and Socializing

For messaging, Brits favor **WhatsApp**, **Facebook Messenger**, **Signal**, **Viber**, and **Telegram**.

When it comes to social media, **Instagram**, **Facebook**, **X**, **TikTok**, and **Reddit** are the most widely used platforms.

If you're new in town and want to meet new people, try **WithLocals**, **EatWith**, and the **Meet Up** website. Looking for love? **Tindr**, **Bumble**, **Hinge**, and **OkCupid** are the most popular dating apps.

Travel and Transportation

Make travel and accommodation bookings (often at discounted rates) on **Booking** and **Expedia**. Other accommodation platforms include **Airbnb** and **Hotels**. Medium-to-long term accommodation can be found on **Spareroom**.

Plan your journeys using **Citymapper**, **Trainline**, and **UK Bus Checker**. In London, the **TFL Go** app is the one you need. For navigation, **Google Maps** and **Waze** will keep from getting lost.

If you need a taxi, local options include **Uber**, **Bolt**, and **Gett**. Hire electric scooters with **Lime**, **Dott**, and **Tier**.

Food and Shopping

Order restaurant meals and groceries for delivery using **Deliveroo**, **Just Eat**, and **Uber Eats**. Additional grocery apps with fast delivery include **Getir**, **Gopuff**, and **Gorillas**.

For general goods, buy online at **Amazon** and **eBay**. Second-hand goods can be had on **Vinted**, **Gumtree**, and **Facebook Marketplace**.

FURTHER READING

Bingham, Harry. *This Little Britain: How One Small Country Changed the Modern World*. London: HarperCollins, 2009.

Bryson, Bill. *Notes from a Small Island*. London: Transworld Publishers, 1995.

Burns, William. *A Brief History of Great Britain*. Infobase Publishing, 2nd edn., 2021.

Davies, John. *A History of Wales*. London: Penguin Books, 2007.

——*The Celts: Prehistory to Present Day*. London: Cassell, 2002.

Dillon, Henry; and Alastair Smith. *Life in the UK Test Handbook 2023: Everything you need to study for the British citizenship test*. Red Squirrel Publishing, 2023.

Fox, Kate. *Watching the English: The Hidden Rules of English Behaviour*. Boston/London: Nicholas Brealey Publishing, revised and updated edition, 2014.

Hirsch, Afua. *Brit(ish): On Race, Identity and Belonging*. New York: Vintage, 2018.

Insight Guides: England. Insight, 2023.

Lewis, Chris; and Penny Mordaunt. *Greater Britain After the Storm*. Biteback Publishing, 2021.

Lonely Planet: Great Britain. Lonely Planet, 2023.

Lyall, Sarah. *The Anglo Files: A Field Guide to the British*. New York: W. W. Norton, 2008.

Madden, Richard. *The Great British Bucket List*. Pavilion Books, 2021.

Marr, Andrew. *A History of Modern Britain*. London: Pan Books, 2017.

Marriott, Emma. *Everything You Really Should Know About GB*. Michael O'Mara, 2015.

Michelin The Green Guide to Scotland. Watford, Herts: Michelin Travel Publications, 12th edn., 2020.

Michelin The Green Guide to Great Britain. Watford, Herts: Michelin Travel Publications, 10th edn., 2018.

Morgan, Kenneth O. *The Oxford History of Britain*. Oxford: University of Oxford Press, revised edition, 2021.

Olusoga, David. *Black and British: A Forgotten History*. Pan Macmillan, 2017.

Paxman, Jeremy. *The English: Portrait of a People*. London: Penguin Books, 2007.

Ross, David. *Scotland: History of a Nation*. Glasgow: Gresham Publishing, 2014.

The Rough Guide to England. Rough Guides, 2023.

Steves, Rick. *Great Britain*. Berkeley, California: Avalon Travel, 24th edn., 2023.

Sanghera, Sathnam. *Empireland: How Imperialism Has Shaped Modern Britain*. New York: Pantheon. 2023.

PICTURE CREDITS

INDEX

Acknowledgment

Special thanks goes to my dad, the brilliant and loving David Riches.